The Saint Monica Club

MAGGIE GREEN

THE SAINT MONICA CLUB

How to Wait, Hope, and Pray for
Your Fallen-Away Loved Ones

SOPHIA INSTITUTE PRESS
Manchester, New Hampshire

Sophia Institute Press
Box 5284, Manchester, NH 03108
1-800-888-9344

www.SophiaInstitute.com

Sophia Institute Press® is a registered trademark of Sophia Institute.

Library of Congress Cataloging-in-Publication Data

Names: Green, Maggie, author.
Title: The Saint Monica Club : how to wait, hope, and pray for your fallen-away loved ones / Maggie Green.
Description: Manchester, New Hampshire : Sophia Institute Press, 2019.
  Summary: "Practical ways to encourage loved ones to return to the Church and to wait patiently for them to do so"— Provided by publisher.
Identifiers: LCCN 2019041301 ISBN 9781622827237 (paperback) ISBN 9781622827244 (ebook)
Subjects: LCSH: Parent and child—Religious aspects—Catholic Church. Parents—Religious life. Reconciliation—Religious aspects—Catholic Church.
Classification: LCC BX2352 .G68 2019 DDC 248.8/45—dc23
LC record available at https://lccn.loc.gov/2019041301

First printing

By a member of
the Saint Monica Club
who lives in hope,
to all other members
who likewise hope for
the day their children return

Contents

What This Book Isn't

Everyone knows someone who is either apathetic or antagonistic toward the Catholic Faith. For those who cherish their faith life and membership in the Catholic Church, it is an open wound, loving someone who, for whatever reason, does not want to come and dine at Christ's table.

Saint Monica prayed, wept, and pleaded with her son and with God for over fifteen years. She stands as a model of both patience and persistence for all of us who have prodigal sons, daughters, friends, and extended family we hope to see one day honored far above us for their devotion to Christ. Saint Monica's son became a Christian, a bishop, and a Doctor of the Church—proof of the power of persistent intercessory prayer, indeed.

Until the day our beloved ones come back to the table, we must likewise persist. It's not easy, it's not fun, but it can be a means of growing closer to God during the watchful waiting time. I wish there were a how-to-get-the-person-you-love-to-return-to-the-Faith-in-ten-easy-steps book, but this is not that book. Method does not bring people to the Faith.

Witness does.

The trick when you have a spouse, friend, child, or relative you love who is far from the Church is—there is no trick. You witness to the Faith by your love, both for your loved one and for God. That's it. That's all. You get to be like the Church, like Christ; always proposing rather than imposing, hoping today, this time, the answer will be, "Yes."

My hope for this book is that it will be a resource for you on how to pray and be steeped in the Faith while you wait in joyful hope. It's designed to provide some consolation to those whose prayers for their children, family, or friends have become a long, aching cry of the heart. Hopefully, it provides strategies for evangelizing the prodigals in your life, while nurturing your own spiritual needs as you weather this waiting time.

There are many of us who pray and weep because, in our weaker moments, we sometimes fear that those we love, or we ourselves, will refuse the invitation to be part of Christ's family by holding on to our hurts and not trusting God to pour out all of His grace to give us every opportunity for salvation. This book is meant to encourage us, to remind us that, as much as we want everyone home at Christmas, Easter, or a birthday, Christ wants our beloved ones home even more.

All of Heaven, all the angels and saints, and Mary, the Blessed Mother of God, are constantly issuing invitations to each of us to come dine with our Lord. They want all of us at the table. All of Heaven is busy preparing the fatted calf for the great feast. I find it a great comfort to know that Jesus wants everyone at the table.

The Saint Monica Club

The Saint Monica Club

Some join for a day, others for a lifetime. Some hold whole handfuls of people they long to see in full reconciliation with Christ. All who become members of this club, however, wish they weren't members. The first step in turning this pain from a defining ache in your heart into an act of giving and prayer, is to name the reality of the hurt.

Being Willing to Cry Out to God, "Lord, the One We Love Is Lost!"

Saint Monica's faith converted both her husband and her son, and it is this steadfastness of faith we seek to imitate. She's the patron saint of parents and spouses who bear the same cross of having someone they love not love the Faith. She knew the pain we know. She prayed and wept and wrestled with it, and she saw God's generous response. She loved her husband and her son through the long desert into the promised land of faith. She loved them before they converted. She loved them through their conversions. She remains the model for all of us, showing us how to weather this storm, not because she suffered but because she loved.

Not being saints, we still struggle with living out that love. It remains a challenge to keep the reality of our loved ones' being far from the Faith in our minds and hearts while letting love guide our actions, words, and thoughts. We keep busy; we try not to rock the boat. Maybe we even allow our prayer lives to diminish in order to trick the estranged persons into thinking we're not so serious in our faith, so that we won't seem like a threat to their professed "anti-faith." Alternatively, perhaps we run through Rosaries like chain smokers. We may offer bargains, grand plans, and promises.

When we love someone who denies, refuses, or ignores the Faith, our own faith is revealed. When someone we love leaves the Faith, we discover all the holes in our own hearts, all the ways in which we haven't fully followed.

I prayed and fasted for a year in the hope that my prodigal would come back to the Church. "No bread but the Eucharist, until she returns," I said. The reasoning felt sound. After all, Jesus told His apostles that some demons leave only through prayer and fasting. It remained an offering at the altar, however, not because God didn't want my child to discover His deep, absolute love for her, but because I had failed to trust God with the offering itself.

I had treated God like an equal. My gift presumed a *quid pro quo*. I do this, and You, God, fix that. But prayer isn't a bargain; it's an act of love. Devoted I might have been, but my prayer and fasting weren't a gift. They were a bribe I hoped would win God over.

Stupid, I know, but pain and sin can make one stupid, and there's no stupidity quite like my "I'm a desperate, frightened, frustrated mother" kind of stupidity. I wanted a quick fix. I wanted my child back. I wanted things to be better but didn't know how to go about it. I knew only how to ask.

Crying out, "Lord, the one we love is lost" applies both to our loved ones and to us, who sometimes lose our way in our struggle for their return. Own this pain, this reality; it hurts because we love. Own it daily in prayer. Members of the Saint Monica Club, persist!

Saint Monica never allowed herself to be satisfied with Saint Augustine's settling for himself, and we're not to settle either. Book 3 of Augustine's *Confessions* tells the following story:

Monica had a vision. She was standing on a wooden beam. A bright, fluorescent being told her to dry her eyes, for "your son is with you." Monica told Augustine about the vision. He responded that, yes, they could indeed be together if she would just abandon her Faith. Monica immediately retorted: "He didn't say that I was with you. He said that you were with me." Augustine never forgot her quick, insightful answer.

We should never forget her quick, insightful answer either. In interacting with someone who is far from the Faith, there's a real temptation to abandon whatever parts of the Faith might cause problems, so as to have some hint of a relationship without friction with the person you love. Settling for a friction-free life, however, is a refusal to love that person or God enough to be willing to suffer. Eventually, it means that our relationships with both God and that person will become a shadow of what they should be. You will become lukewarm and will neither win your prodigal's soul for God nor prove yourself to be a true disciple.

So keep the prayer in your heart and return to it daily, asking for that person's full return to the Faith. Call upon Saint Monica to pray with you. Ask her to pray for you as well, because she knows how hard the long wait is. She also knows the wait is worth it.

There Are No Quick Fixes

Most of us know Saint Monica as the mother of Doctor of the Church Saint Augustine. For more than seventeen years, Saint Monica wept, prayed, and counseled her son and asked others to pray for him. Seventeen years of tears! More than a decade and a half of seeking out bishops and priests, of prayers, of talking to her son about what she had raised him to be. Our modern culture doesn't quite comprehend such holy persistence, but Monica is a perfect model for us.

I concede that I often pray to God with an impatient heart: "How about today?" "Now?" "Pretty please?" I complain, "It's been more than a year. When, Lord? When?" But I know that all time belongs to God. The Israelites wandered for forty years in the desert, having suffered more than four hundred years in captivity. And all the world held its breath, waiting, trusting God's promise, for Mary's fiat, for the night of Christmas, for Good Friday, and for Easter and Pentecost. God's time is not our time, and it's sometimes hard to remember that when we'd really like our prayer answered yesterday.

I've sometimes whined at God over His timing on this matter. If God wants it, why isn't it already done?

The answer?

God has already acted, and He continues to act. He became man, He became a creature, He willed Himself on the Cross, and He's still offering Himself in every Mass as the Eucharist. He's willing to take the form of even inanimate things (bread and wine) to get Himself into our hearts. He has been crucified to win us back. He's willing to knock on each of our hearts until we answer.

Knowing that God's ways are not our ways and living it are two different things. "Thy will be done" is not for the faint of heart; it is the prayer of our Lord and echoes Mary's fiat, "Let it be done to me according to your word." Those words would be hard for us to repeat if we did not know that our God is love. There's comfort in knowing that as much as we desire our children to come home, God wants it even more. God loves them more than we can ever dream. He created them for love. He created them for eternal communion with Him. If our hearts howl with longing for them to be at the dinner table or in the pew with us, how much more does our heavenly Father long and groan for each of His children to be willing to rest in His heart?

Over and over again, I need the reminder in my own heart: God wants it more. He has already done what is needed to ransom our souls from sin and death. All we need to do is cooperate with His will. It's easy to see how someone else is not cooperating with God; it's much harder to see how we ourselves are not. Trusting God's grace to act in our lives and in the lives of those we hold dear—that's surrendering control to God. It remains a daily offering we must make. We must diminish. We must make room for God to work, pulling away at the roof of our souls and trusting always that God acts and that He longs for this reunion, always and everywhere, infinitely more than we do. Repeat as often as needed: I am not in charge. I am here to love and to cooperate with God's will, to assist in teaching the rest of the world about God's great, infinite, merciful love by my own obedience and my own witness of that same gift.

Sitting at the Feet of Jesus
Is Doing Something

As part of the grieving process, I registered for an online program to learn how to cope, but I found it too generic. My child's walking away wasn't one issue; it was many, all mixed together. I couldn't argue or engage; I could only endure.

Guilt struck me hard. Had we failed? Where? When?

Combing through the years, I sought to find the moment, the failure point upon which it all hinged. I found all of them and none. There wasn't an "Aha!" moment, but I came to the simple realization that free will is a vexing reality in all God's children. Theoretically, we had done everything we were supposed to—going to church on Sundays, praying, explaining what needed explaining when the occasion arose, sending them to Catholic schools—and, yet, here my own were, walking away.

Because I'm an enthusiastic person, I sought to "do something," so I read articles and looked for groups addressing this issue, but I found none that fit the bill. There are support groups for grief, for depression, for caring for a person with an addiction, for weathering all sorts of sufferings, but there isn't (as far as I could find) a ministry for those who are hoping one day to find their children within their Father's house.

Part of the reason for this lack is that the world doesn't acknowledge the problem of a fallen-away child as something one should ache or weep over. Questioning one's faith and testing it remains part of growing up and a necessary part of becoming a spiritually mature adult. The world celebrates the abandonment of faith, however, and any parent or family member who grieves the loss of faith is painted as someone who is repressed, trying to impose values and to control the estranged person's life choices. At best, the world considers every religion equal to another or, more often, inferior to the nuanced decision to embrace no religion. Ergo, the world puzzles, "Why grieve if a child or adult rejects his Faith? Isn't that merely proof of his being independent?" The world would tell us we're upset over nothing. As long as our kids remain healthy physically and self-sufficient economically, this faith business is an add-on, a bonus, not a necessity.

The world does not love our children, however, not as we love and certainly not as God loves. The fallen nature of the world would tell us not to worry about our children's loss of faith, but anyone who loves knows that indifference is the exact opposite of love. We do not want our children merely to exist but to live, and not merely live but to thrive in love. We need salt and light, or the world remains tasteless and dark. We want our children to be that salt and light to others, to be disciples of Christ. The reality that they're not, that they're not even seeking Him, hurts.

Everyone who loves someone else wills that person's good. If we love anyone, we will that person's permanent happiness, and the only place permanent, divine happiness can be found is with God. Everyone hopes and strives for their beloved ones to discover the ultimate source of happiness, joy, and peace, whether or not they know it's God. To quote Saint Monica's son, "Our hearts are restless until they rest in Thee." It's true for our prodigals and for us also. Our own hearts are restless because we know that our loved ones' hearts are not resting in the Lord. But that's our hope and thus our prayer. That's the whole reason we ache. That's the whole reason we are members of this club. We are praying; we are hoping for our children to find themselves deeply in love with the One who is Love.

We are the Church; therefore, we are the Club. We are the support group for each other in this pilgrimage to our true home. We've got the friendship of our Lord and of all His angels and saints, including Saint Monica, who, as our patroness, will teach us how to be both relentless in prayer and patient with our prodigals.

Still want to "do something"? Sit in front of the Blessed Sacrament or with Scripture. Sit at the feet of Jesus. When you feel yourself growing anxious about the matter, about your prodigal, run to the tabernacle. Why? Because Jesus tells us what He tells His friend Martha: "Martha, Martha, you are anxious and worried about many things." And He points to her sister Mary, who has chosen the better portion by sitting at the feet of Jesus and listening to Him (Luke 10:38–42). Choosing the better portion is doing something. It is the best thing we can do, bringing all our woes to the feet of Jesus and listening to His Sacred Heart. What we hear whispered from the tabernacle we can repeat in the everyday, ordinary part of life to the ears of those we hope will truly hear. Our hearts will be restless until our hearts (our prodigal children) rest in Thee.

Do Something Loving

What do we do now? If our child, our parent, our friend, or even a stranger were drowning, we wouldn't simply insist, "God, save that person!" We'd search for a life preserver. We'd cry out for help. We'd jump in to help the person. We cannot wash our hands and say, "He's an adult" or "She's made up her mind."

Having a prodigal you love means more work, not less.

Dropping to our knees and praying is active, deliberate work —work we're required to do both as parents who promised at our children's baptisms to bring them up in the Faith and as stewards entrusted with these talents we're supposed to multiply. We want to hear, "Well done, good and faithful servant." So roll up your sleeves. The hard work of loving begins on your knees.

Many of us (myself included) thought potty training, dealing with adolescence, and paying for college were the hard parts of parenting. These trials prepared us, but the more important part of the race, the task of loving our children and being prayer warriors for them all the way into Heaven, remains. It's not something we consider when we're pouring out everything during the early years, when our lives are consumed with the mere manual labor of sustaining our children day after day. It's not something we belabor in the middle years, when we worry: Have we pushed them enough or too much? Have we educated them well? Have we given them a foundation?

When they leave home, if we've done all they need for physical, social, and economic survival, the world says we've served them well. If this is all we've done, though, then we've merely banged cymbals and clanged gongs. We have a solemn duty to introduce our children to God by our words, our deeds, and, yes, by our witness to the Faith. We can do all of this, and still, our whole job is merely to prepare their hearts and sow the seed; it is God's grace that will bring forth the fruits.

When our children were babies, we understood that we were to have servants' hearts for them. That reality has not changed in subsequent years; only the way we serve has. We must continue to illustrate God's love and our willingness to be used by God to love. Loving your prodigals, no matter how challenging they might be or how old, is learning how to imitate God the Father by imitating God the Son. We willingly sacrifice our hands and feet, our head and our side; we offer ourselves, or we do not love.

We must always work to love even more. Even if your child will not suffer your presence, continue to serve if only through prayer, if only by offering your own pain in penance. Love is a form of praying without ceasing. We are never done loving. We are never done praying either. Moreover, that servant's heart we're to have isn't limited to our children; it's formed to serve all our brothers and sisters in Christ.

Be Kind, Not Nice

In families where tensions exist owing to an estrangement of one or more members from the Faith, we often try to cloak special occasions and even ordinary conversation in the false peace of manners. "Please" and "thank you" and conversations that touch only on the safest of subjects project the veneer of domestic tranquility. If the talk strays even a little, however, explosions occur.

Being truly kind requires bravery. Kindness is truth delivered with mercy; service freely given. We cannot be witnesses to our Faith if we fear rejection, nor are we to go about using our Faith like a battering ram. Be unfailingly kind on all occasions, to all people, and you will reveal to your prodigal an uncompromising principle of love. That's the goal. The rule is to avoid being either the fire starter or the fanner of flames. You must be a source of peace, even when it might be your heart's desire to fight, to push back, or to argue.

Nothing undermines witness like losing one's temper. Such firestorms strip all prior acts of gentleness of their true intent in the eyes of the other person. Any kindness now seems deliberate and manipulative, designed to win the person over with niceness. We know we cannot manipulate if we are to love. We also cannot even appear to manipulate if our love is to be perceived.

Understand that the false peace created through manners merely creates an artificial veneer, an illusion that everything is fine. When a family is struggling with a prodigal, everyone knows that everything is not fine — especially the prodigal.

When your prodigal is visiting, include him or her in the ordinary. Your prodigal is not a special guest who must be catered to but someone you love and who presumably loves you. So be real. Invite him or her to help with the planning of the dinner or the dishes or to watch a movie with you afterward. Keeping your loved one at safe or pre-arranged distances at all times will not facilitate either your relationship with your loved one or his or her relationship with God.

At the table, the silence of whatever it is that is not being discussed is not peaceful. It's a high-tension, emotional tightrope that will make all your family members hold their breath, hoping just to get through the meal. Talk about memories, about fun things. Ask questions that encourage a free exchange of ideas without necessarily jumping to core issues, allowing all the family to participate. Ask for ideas for movies, for activities for the next day or for the summer. This will be a reminder for you and your child that you can relate to each other despite differences, because love and trust are built on joy, on shared experiences, and on hearing what the other has to say. The core issues remain, yes, but the goal in this circumstance is to deepen your relationship with each other, and that can happen through little things done with great love.

One of my most painful moments (when I didn't get a job I had been hoping for) turned into a beautiful treasure when my prodigal took me for a walk to let me weep and to remind me that I'm still blessed, even suggesting, despite professed unbelief, that I pray. That was truly a gift, and it would never have happened if I had triumphed. Real life lived with those you love, whether they believe or not, may lead you to a deeper faith when you least expect it and reveal something of theirs in the process.

Manners are not kindness; they are nice. Kindness is an offering of the self. Niceness is a cloaking of feelings beneath civility, protocol, and etiquette. We're called to be kind, not nice. So above all, in all things, be kind. It's the best witness. It's the honest witness that will win hearts, and, in fact, it's the only way to witness.

The Daily Surrender

When we love someone who does not know God, who struggles with having a relationship with us because of God, it becomes our mission to be for that person a reflection of God's love in all things. Offering ourselves over and over again for our prodigals, as an imitation of Christ's love, is the essence of "white martyrdom." Let yourself be drained dry, wrung out for Christ. This offering of self can, however, sometimes get warped by our ego, our impatience, or our inability to stay in God's grace when faced with friction, rebukes, or pain. Every day we must begin again.

Remember, you have always loved your prodigal, and you're called always to love him or her more deeply. Look at the person you love as you did when all you could do was drink in his or her eyes. This is your child. This is your beloved. This is a person for whom you would willingly sacrifice everything. In some way, you're to love this person who wants a reason to reject love utterly. You must do your best not to give one, not by being safe but by being kind.

Hold your child in your heart if you cannot hold him or her in the flesh. Place your child in your heart as if placing the Eucharist in the tabernacle. Place your child on the altar as you would the gifts. Give him or her back to God at every Mass, in every Rosary, and in every prayer. You are practicing a form of detachment that parallels Mary's in offering her Son at the Temple in the Presentation (Luke 2:22–24). You are surrendering your claim on this child in favor of God's. It's not easy. It is, however, necessary.

The surrender of our grasp on our children's future may, in fact, be how our souls are claimed for God, because they rest no longer on their own merit but on God's grace. Our prodigals may be the means by which we come to love God and trust Him more and ourselves less.

We know from experience that all service is tedious and irksome. But love makes it possible, and perfect love makes it a joy. Also, we know that howsoever we judge, so we shall be judged. So, love as you wish to be loved, without counting the hours or the effort. Do the little and the big things with great love so that there's no room for anything else.

Ask for Help

The hardest part of loving someone estranged from the Faith is the sense of isolation. As I said, there are no support groups for those grieving the loss of a family member from the Faith. This loneliness is no accident. It is the Devil's design to make not only your child but you, too, feel cut off from God. You will need people with whom you can walk, pray, and weep when it gets hard. You will need wise people who tell you when you're being pushy or when you need to speak up. You will need people to bolster your courage, to feed your spirit when it feels quenched, and to pray for your beloved and for you. You will need both heavenly and earthly friends as part of your support system.

So, cry out to Heaven. Heaven will not fail to answer. Make friends with Saint Monica, who knows your ache. Make friends with Saint Anthony, and ask him to help you find a way to relate to your child and to help your child find his or her way home. Ask Saint Peter to help your child become a close friend of Jesus. Ask Saint Paul to give you the words and Saint James to tell you when to be silent. Ask Saint Augustine and Saint Thomas for convincing arguments when they must be made. Ask Saint Thérèse of Lisieux and Saint Teresa of Calcutta how to do little things with great love. Ask your children's guardian angels to watch over them, and ask yours to watch over you. In short, make friends with the company of saints, and if you have favorite saints, put them on notice. Find new ones to add to the list. Pick a mystery of the Rosary that fits with the personality of the person you are praying for, and make that your loved one's special mystery.

Ask all your departed relatives to pray for your child. Ask the souls in Purgatory, and offer your pain for them. Ask your child's patron saints, godparents, Confirmation saint and Confirmation sponsor. Ask your pastor. Ask your bishop. Write the pope. Ask your friends online. You need not mention specifics; simply ask them to pray for a special intention. Light candles in churches. Be like the woman in the Gospel, pestering the unjust judge, seeking a ruling. God, who is the Just Judge, will use your asking to great effect. So, ask often. Ask again and again and again and again.

Part of trusting God is knowing what Jesus tells us: "Knock, and the door will be opened. Seek and you will find" (see Matt. 7:7). So, ask your heavenly Father to bring your child into the fullness of faith, to give your child a heart for love alone. Make it a daily request. This constant petition will nourish your relationship with the citizens of Heaven and with God. It will nourish your friendships here on Earth as well. You won't feel alone anymore, and you'll realize that you never were.

Persist and know that while you may weary of asking, God never wearies of being asked. I take great comfort in nagging the Almighty with my prayers. As I told a friend long ago, "I'm always unreasonable with God. He's the only one I can be unreasonable with." Ask for the unreasonable. God specializes in the miraculous, resplendent, glorious, joyful, and lavish. Trust that the answer will be luminous. Heaven will answer. Heaven seeks all of us.

Keep Inviting Them In,
through Every Door
You Can Find

There's a strong temptation, when your heart feels pained by a child's rejection of the Faith, to begin to define your relationship either entirely around that rejection or exclusively apart from that component of life. Neither is a correct response. We do not relate to anyone via one lens only, unless we do not want any real relationship with the individual at all.

Your child's restored relationship with Christ may come through strengthening his or her relationship with you. Any love given and received is God's love; ergo, whatever love you build and strengthen between you and your adult child is a reflection of God's love for both of you. So, don't make your every conversation about the Faith, but at the same time, don't shy away from discussing the Faith when the situation calls for it.

"Will you come with us to Mass? Your sister is singing." This is an invitation, both to a place for an event and to witness a sibling participate. Sometimes, a sideways door allows a prodigal to enter in, to experience something of what that person has removed himself or herself from, and sometimes, that little visit is all God needs.

On the other hand, insisting that someone come will likely lead to shouting matches and the very opposite of a compelling witness to the importance of a relationship with Christ. Your child may not come with you to Sunday Mass, but that doesn't mean that your child doesn't get to hear what the rest of your family thought about the homily or the Gospel when you sit down to breakfast.

The Church never imposes; she proposes. So, too, the domestic church must propose (as a lover) to the lost sheep of the family if we are to win them over eventually with love.

We also still have to allow for that pesky free will and the very real likelihood of a no. We know that "love hopes all things," (1 Cor. 13:7), and so, our job as parents of a prodigal is always to leave the door open, always to ask. One day, the answer might be yes. If you don't know when to ask or how to go about it, ask the Holy Spirit to guide you. "The Holy Spirit will teach you in that very hour what you ought to say" (Luke 12:12). All three persons of the Trinity are involved in seeking the salvation of each soul: the Holy Spirit, hoping to awaken the soul's deepest desire; Christ, offering Himself as a sacrament; and the Father, seeking to welcome each soul home with all that He has. If we need a model of how we are to act, speak, and love when encountering a prodigal in our lives, it is the Blessed Trinity. All three persons of God are engaged in this very real courtship of every soul, for we are all prodigals in desperate need of being led home. If we know this is true of God, who is perfect, then it makes it easier for us, who are not perfect, to endure the long wait in our own courtship of other souls.

That patience becomes all the more critical when a rift forms from the spiritual break within a family. Some seek to battle it, others to accommodate it, and still others to weather it. But the environment can grow toxic and confrontational to the point that it pierces the whole family like a nail. The absence of love where love should be is an Agony in the Garden for all afflicted, for all who want reconciliation but don't know how to go about it. Fortunately, we can take action.

Pray. In the heat of things, it feels as if the crisis in your family life will go on infinitely, but it can't, so it won't. Pray for strength to endure the temptation to believe that your family life will never be better, never be healed. (That's the Devil's way of getting you to stop praying, stop hoping, stop trusting in God's grace to prevail.) Kneeling before the crucifix, look at the wounds of Christ. Peer into the openings holding the nails. One family member is the nail on the left, and the other on the right, both connected by the body and the blood of Jesus and both entrenched, refusing to budge.

It is then that the Heart of the One who loves both is pierced. It is then that we must remember the words of our Lord: "Truly, I say to you, whoever says to this mountain, 'Be taken up and cast into the sea,' and does not doubt in his heart, but believes that what he says will come to pass, it will be done for him" (Mark 11:23). When a family is separated by anger, by pain, by time, by hurt over hurt over hurt, prayer doesn't need to move just one mountain but many, perhaps a whole range, requiring a spiritual tectonic plate shift. You who love them, ask for the mountains to move, and prepare for an avalanche of grace.

Keep Living Life and
Sharing What You Know

Like faith without works, prayer without works is dead. We can't be mere petitioners of God. We must be participators in the working out of our salvation. So, when we're not serving our children, when we're not petitioning Heaven, what else should we do?

Get outside your own head and your home. Go into the world and live. God made us to be stewards of each other and all others. If you cannot minister directly to your adult children (because they won't let you or they're not proximate), care for others around you who will let you. Be a source of light and strength to others. Practice the spiritual and corporal works of mercy in earnest, anchoring them in the point of pain in your own life. Make it personal. For example, if your child suffers from an eating disorder (either not eating or being a glutton), feed the hungry. If your child suffers from an addiction, find a ministry for those addicted. If your child struggles with a philosophical type of estrangement, become a teacher of your own Faith. Bone up on the more than two thousand years of brilliant minds within the Catholic tradition who wrestled with the questions "Who is

Christ?" and "Who are we called to be?" Growing in knowledge of the Faith is a way of witnessing.

We don't need to join every apostolate, but we should use this time of tears as a means of developing stronger spiritual roots. We'll need that strength to deal with others in our families who might have been influenced by our prodigal children to consider straying themselves. A deeper understanding of the Faith will also serve to keep our own spiritual lives from being eroded by fatigue or attacks. God always calls each of us deeper and deeper in. None of us are finished discovering God's deep and abiding love.

Often, the estrangement of a loved one is what brings those of us who love that person deeper and deeper in, and we discover the shallowness of our understanding of the faith and of our roots in it.

Every joy and every suffering is an invitation to fall more deeply in love with God, if only we recognize the opportunity. When we are at peace, it is time to glorify God for His generosity. When we are in pain, we are invited to participate in Christ's Passion. When we are overwhelmed, we know something of God's willingness to shoulder all our burdens; and when we are blessed, we remember that ours is a generous and loving God who desires only for us to know and love His company.

Meet Them Where They Are

So far, we've discussed the reality of having adult children who have walked away from the Faith, but what about when the conflict remains in front of you? What about the teens who won't go to Mass, or the college students who reject the Church's teachings on sexuality, or the adults who lead lives contrary to the Faith and still live at home? "Love your children where they are" sounds lovely until you have to put it into practice and come up against realities you find objectionable.

Remember that Jesus meets the woman at the well and calls to Zacchaeus in his tree. He calls to Matthew at his customs post and to James and John as they work with their father on the fishing nets. He comes to each of us where we are. Sometimes, after we have been evangelized, we can forget what it feels like to be one who has yet to hear in the heart God's invitation. Our job is to make sure we aren't drowning out God's invitation. Jesus asked people what they wanted of Him: "What do you want me to do for you?" The blind man said, "I want to see" (see Mark 10:51). Jesus seeks out each of us individually through our lives, through our sufferings, our joys, and our relationships. Make sure you're letting Him speak through you with the invitation to something more, something whole, something holy.

Begin by listening to your prodigal, wherever that child is in his or her faith journey, and affirming whatever is good. It may require homework to find out what parallels and differences exist between Catholicism and the possible creed embraced by your child. Wherever he or she is, find what good is in it and proclaim it. If your child has gone to another faith, ask your child to share his or her faith journey, to explain what he or she knows about it. Do your homework, too, not so you can cross-examine but so you can really know what your child is and is not embracing.

If your child has dropped faith as a premise (like many of this age, self-professed "Nones"), again, look for what your child is doing that reveals what he or she values. Is your child attracted to beauty? A seeker of justice? Seeking and desiring fellowship? Serving others and wanting a better society? Look at the substitutes for God your child has adopted — again, not to cross-examine or to prove, "Aha! You've created a golden calf," but to understand how God is still reaching for your child, still speaking to the soul to win it over.

We are to see as Saint Paul saw the early Greeks and their temple to the Unknown God, to look at our children's lives and meet them where they are. "Men of Athens, I see that in every way, you are religious" (Acts 17:22). Pope Benedict XVI spoke lovingly of those who professed and adhered to other creeds and of all of humanity's groping for God, seeking to see and know Him: image seeking the Divine who created the image, heart seeking the Divine Heart. We can do no less.

What if your child rejects it all? If your child is open to discussion, ask him to write out his objections to the Faith, not because you're preparing a legal brief to refute them but so you can examine the root of the problem. Perhaps there are writings that address the particular issues from sources your prodigal hasn't seen. Even if your child is not open to reading or examining these sources, it's good for you to read them to bolster your faith.

Don't apologize for believing what your child does not, but do become someone who can, if need be, give a good defense of why you believe. If someone comes at you about abortion, you need to be able to say, "I want to protect the mother, the father, and the child, and so I will not sacrifice any one of them for the others' convenience. I want the dignity of all of them preserved." Say that you believe that dignity is innate and that you believe human life begins at conception. If the objection is over birth control pills, talk about how the medication breaks a working body for the purposes of gratifying another and about how it dampens and injures the pleasure and joy of sex for the woman. You will have to know what the objections are and what the standard arguments against your position are if you are to give a good defense. Don't seek the argument, though. Merely train yourself to be able to hold your position from a place of knowledge and understanding. Conversion rarely comes through winning an argument, so do not think of your studying as a means to triumph intellectually, but rather as a means to witness more knowledgeably.

If your loved one is an atheist or an agnostic, you can still bring that person to witness something of God in the extraordinary. Begin with the beauty of creation. Creation is God's cathedral. Beauty invites the person experiencing it to be in awe, to experience wonder, and to engage in contemplation. It can be the ocean, a mountain, the stars, the moon, the forest, or some creature, but the easiest way for any of us to recognize that we aren't the center of the universe is to discover how remarkable, large, beautiful, and complex the universe is. Awe of beauty is an imitation of wonder and awe of God, the Imaginer and Creator of that beauty. All of Heaven and Earth sings of the glory of God. We just need to keep providing opportunities to hear the singing. Plant a garden or a tree or help clean up a river. These things seem very physical and secular, but they're a means by which God speaks without using words. God knows we need the physical to understand that which is beyond physical, so all of Earth is a doorway to Heaven, if we learn to see it and love it for what it reflects.

Service of others, too, brings anyone who lives it into the presence of God. Relieving something of the suffering of the world allows a person to encounter Christ in His distressing disguise while being the hands and feet of Christ without necessarily knowing it. That person might be one of those who says, "Lord, Lord, when did I ever see you hungry or thirsty?" to which our Lord will say, "As you did to the least of these, you did unto me" (see Matt. 25:37, 40). If you can, volunteer with your fallen-away family member. Work side by side, and let God do the orchestrating, which sometimes takes a lifetime or might happen in an instant. If the prodigal is not interested in volunteering, do it yourself, and offer your sacrifice of time, effort, and service in reparation for injuries done to Christ. If nothing else, it will serve as a reminder and a witness to the Faith and prove that it isn't simply a creed or set of moral principles to be embraced, but the way to live life more fully.

Keep your home a place of faith by prayer, sacramentals, and traditions and by always inviting the prodigal one to join you. Do not hide your belief, but do not push it either. Live it, and cultivate in yourself a willingness to be seen praying without making a show of it. It can be reading Scripture, praying the Rosary, going to Adoration, or all three, but let your child see that this isn't a hobby, a mindless custom, or a tradition; it's an important part of your life. This isn't necessary only for your child; it's also part of keeping you from feeling drained while waiting, like salt that loses its flavor. Spend this time trimming your lamp with oil, fattening your soul on the feast of the sacraments and all that the Church offers. Be like Joseph in the Old Testament, storing up grain for the years of famine so as to be able to weather them. There may be famine years to come. Just know that the feast will eventually happen, so keep yourself ready to prepare the fatted calf.

Take Up the Cross by
Treating Others with Dignity
in All Things

Sometimes you will be mocked. Sometimes you will be hated. Sometimes you will be told you are positively wrongheaded in all things. How does one deal with challenging issues such as abortion, birth control, same-sex "marriage," cohabitation, and pornography when the world dismisses as puritanical and bigoted all standards other than one's own appetite? How do we deal with the anger that builds both from what is not discussed and from what is? How do we hold fast to love and not let our values be eroded or viewed as mere matters of preference?

These are not easy questions, and although the answer is simple, living it isn't. Being Catholic means loving beyond what is safe and, ultimately, being willing to suffer with Christ and possibly suffer like Christ in our lives. No one likes hearing, "Take up your cross," but it's necessary. Take up this cross like a lover, and follow. You will answer your prodigal by how you live your life. Witnessing to a life of dignity in all areas requires that you treat *everyone* as having innate dignity and having been made in God's image and that you not merely "endure the slings and arrows of outrageous fortune" but suffer well (that is, with grace). Christ tells us again and again that we are to love God first with all our heart, with all that we are, and to love our neighbor as ourselves. This means we must always speak to all people through the filter of our Faith and with love. We must provide truth steeped in charity and wisdom laced with peace. We must serve others in all things with mercy, both spiritual and corporal.

Those words sound really pretty until you have to live them. Living them means being willing to explain: this is why we don't have birth control, we don't allow pornography, we don't condone abortion, and we don't believe in casual sex or sex between unmarried people or any sex outside the context of a sacramental union. We view sex as sacred and an outward sign of an internal reality, the union created between a man and a woman by God in full witness of the Church. "Be ready to give a defense" means it's time to do your homework and to learn that every day you can live out your Faith more.

We have all these "rules" as manifestations of a fundamental belief that all people have innate dignity. The modern world views holding a standard as equal to condemning someone. But the Church teaches something timeless: we are made in equal dignity and in God's image, male and female. Some of these things will be hard to say, and some of them will be hard for your child to hear. Ask the Holy Spirit for guidance about when to speak and when to witness by your life. Ask God for the words before speaking or instructing. Be obedient when the still, small voice in your heart says, "Speak" and when it says, "Be still."

So, if your adult child is engaged in behavior that troubles you, focus on your child's innate dignity and the dignity of whoever he or she associates with, and let that vision of their innate dignity and infinite worth help you to relate to whoever comes into your home. Pray, "Jesus, let me love as You love, see as You see, serve as You would have me serve." And trust God to give you both the inspiration and the will to cooperate. You can draw a line. You can say, "We can't have this in our home because we have small children." You can say what you won't support, but be able to explain why and, above all, do so with full charity.

If the prodigal still wants to engage in an intellectual battle of ethics or morals, offer the suggestion of going for a hike or a drive so that the discussion is removed from distractions and from others who might not hear anything but the tone or who might not be ready to hear these more philosophical and difficult conversations. Keep the conversation anchored in ideas, rather than on specific people and behaviors, and discuss the "why" of things and the consistency of your faith, which is based not on a political ideology but on knowing Christ, loving Christ, and seeking to follow Christ in all things. When discussing the tough topics, it's all right to point out that the root of these problematic issues is often a desire to do what one wants or to allow others to do as they will. Liberty without restriction is license, but that's a hard sell to anyone who wants not merely permission, but approval of all actions.

How does one address such issues without being either a fire-and-brimstone type or a doormat? Let your child talk first. Listen. Listen to what is said and what is not said. Hearing the "why" and understanding your child's motivation will perhaps help you to offer a solution, one that may render some of the arguments against the Faith less potent. If nothing else, listening, really listening and taking in the point of view of your prodigal will allow you to reflect on where he or she is spiritually and give you something of a spiritual map showing what you need to pray for. Listening will in no way injure your relationship with them.

It does, however, take sublimation of the self and the very real desire to "win" in the conversation.

Evangelization of strangers begins with connecting on a personal level, with a relationship. Evangelization of our own children, spouses, and other family members begins at the same place. Ask them questions. Ask them to ask questions. There might be cut-and-dried issues about which you cannot agree, but the reality is that you have to begin where your prodigal is, rather than where you hope he or she will one day be. You must remain willing to be patient, to be kind, and to find where you and your prodigal agree in order to do the hard work of building a bridge from that starting point.

Rejection of the Faith often stems from a confused view of the tenets of the Faith as prohibitions on our freedom. What the world views as restrictions are actually God's laws designed to save us from becoming slaves to sin and its consequence, death. If you cannot stop someone from being a slave to whatever appetite has that person in the grips of addiction—be it fame, pleasure, honor, wealth, power, or glory—then be the reminder of what a life without addiction to sin looks like. Be a joyful mystery, a revelation by your love of what is better than all the world offers. If you are joyful in your ordinary life, it is hard to argue that you've chosen anything poorly. If you are revealing virtue as a source of joy (restraint, success with diets or budgets), discipline (becoming more accomplished in a new skill), humble (when others would be proud), you make those who know you, who see what you are not doing, curious about how it is possible. A joyous couple with a child or several children is a testimony to a couple without children about what they may be missing. A joyful adult caring for an elderly friend reminds others, by his or her witness in the world, of the need for such kindness and care on a regular basis. When we are generous, it prompts others to consider whether they ought to be more generous as well. So feed the hungry, house the homeless, comfort the lonely, be the source of God's abundant mercy for your prodigal. A good teacher in graduate school drilled into my head, "All behavior is communication." It's your job to listen to what your prodigal has to say (or to be aware of your prodigal's silence on certain matters) and to respond by saying and doing something that reveals love.

So, love your family member with everything you have, and ask for God to give you more grace so that you won't fall into either frustration — "I've loved you, so why haven't you changed?" (treating love as a bribe) — or despair — "I don't want to give anymore" (rendering your love finite or conditional). Jesus calls us to love as He loves. It's not easy. It's a cross we're being offered, to love someone more than we thought we could, simply because that person exists. If you need further encouragement, just look to Jesus. Jesus looked with love at the young man who kept all the commandments. Jesus, likewise, did not condemn the woman caught in adultery and tells us in no uncertain terms that neither should we condemn. We're to be like Jesus and keep offering opportunities for people to begin again, just as God the Father does for us each time we come to receive the Eucharist, each time we partake of the sacrament of Reconciliation, each time we go on our knees and try once again, to get closer to Christ.

Being an Attractive Witness to Marriage and the Family

It's heartbreaking to know that your child willfully exhibits destructive behavior, whatever it is. But if you remain silent so as to avoid being judgmental, your silence may be interpreted as acceptance.

It is not condemnation to hold that you don't want anyone to use anyone else or to view anyone else as a disposable pleasure or an object. It's not contemptuous to hold that you will not condone behavior that reduces the dignity of men and women, even if those involved consent to do so. Being faithful to the teachings of the Church is a call to deal with others according to their true value.

In an age when the highest requirement of a relationship is consent, the Church holds up a better standard: fidelity, permanence, and willingness to sacrifice oneself. The Church has what people want, what people buy magazines by the ton to try to find through techniques and easy tips. The Church holds the key to relationships that last, that matter, that grow. Witnessing to this reality by your own example is the most compelling way to win a heart.

An authentic witness to the goodness of the family is radiant, beautiful, and attractive. Our world is starving for such a witness. Anyone who has ever met an elderly couple quietly and deeply in love, seen a young mother gazing at her baby, or heard parents cheering for their son for finishing a race has witnessed this genuine beauty, the joy of willing only the good of the other.

The essence of the Christian life is to learn how to reveal God's love to the world through how we live. Begin with your own marriage and your own understanding of the catechism. Have you allowed the Faith to permeate your whole life? Steep your marriage in the values you hope to uphold. Ask yourself the hard questions: Does my marriage reflect a belief in the innate dignity of man and woman, the sacramental nature of sex within the confines of such a union (permanent, sacrificial, faithful, and open to life)? If not, why not? Wherever it is not sacrificial, wherever your faith is confined rather than expressed, this is your starting point. Begin by discussing with your spouse what you want your marriage and family to look like. Ask how you can get there and what steps need to be taken. Discuss why it hasn't happened yet or what the stumbling block has been.

Stumbling blocks in faith reveal to us how we, too, are prodigals who think ourselves the older brother in the parable. If there aren't any places where you're wrestling with the Faith, ask God to show you where you fall short, what you aren't doing. We should know from Scripture and from our own experience that God will multiply whatever we offer. God wants to break into our lives and the lives of our prodigals even more. Offer what you can, and prepare to have your life cracked open, expanded beyond what you thought possible.

Next, get to the homework of knowing the Faith. Knowing the "why" of things will help you discuss them. Why is the Church against abortion, artificial birth control, and so forth. Read the catechism so you may begin to understand the teachings of the Church, not as rigid rules to obey but as natural extensions of the deeper, fuller meaning of Jesus' words to the Pharisees: "Love your God with your whole heart, and your neighbor as yourself" (see Luke 10:27).

Whether you are a parent, a sibling, a spouse, or a friend of a prodigal, you need to know the deeper reasoning, the Holy Spirit–infused understanding behind these teachings, both to give a good account of Catholicism and to follow it better yourself. The more you know of what accounts for sacred tradition and sacred teaching, the better you can defend it. Don't be fooled, however, by thinking you can argue your loved one into conversion. (That seldom works.) But with this knowledge, you can give a response when part of your Faith is attacked, either by your prodigal's questions or his actions. It also helps to solidify your own spiritual life so that you can be sure your house is built on a strong foundation.

There Will Always Be a Test

Some prodigals seek more than to leave the Faith; they seek to convert. They don't just reject; they defect from the Faith, in part, as an affirmation of the rejection itself. If your beloved wants to reduce the Faith to its past, poor witnesses, mistakes, grave sins, current scandals, and so forth, remind him or her that you remain Catholic not because Catholics are perfect but because you know that what the Church teaches is true. You aren't a member of the Church to make friends or to make the world a better place but to know God and to be made a better person, through the medicine offered in the sacraments, through Scripture, and through all the wisdom, writings, and witnesses of all the saints and martyrs. You don't view the Church as an ancient institution but as the Bride of Christ, the Body of Christ, and the means of coming to know and love God more fully.

There will always be a test. It will always be pass or fail, and your only job in these pop quizzes of life, whether at the dinner table or while listening to the car radio with your prodigal, is to respond with love and, if possible, humor. There's a story I love about a high school senior who encountered atheists in the hallway on his way to class every day. During Holy Week, he walked the gauntlet, and they taunted, "God is dead. God is dead. God is dead." He turned and quipped, "That happens on Friday." They stopped mocking him after that week.

Humor is an underutilized tool for both evangelization and de-escalating difficult or tense situations. It's hard to hate or to ignore people who make you laugh, who don't take themselves so seriously, even when the subjects being discussed are serious. An attractive witness is one who isn't angry at himself or anyone else. Humor is a sign of humility. So be humble. Laugh when things get too hard to handle seriously, and you can be certain that you'll pass whatever test comes up.

Your Job Is to Inform and Witness, Not to Persuade

Let's say you've explained what you believe and why you believe it. Let's say you've taught your children the catechism, taken them to Mass, and witnessed to the Faith in your life, and still they've opted to reject some of the teachings of the Faith, or they've walked away entirely. What then?

You must simply continue to be a steady witness, a reminder, and a source of salt and light in your prodigal's life by what you do, what you say, and through prayer and sacrifice. Saint Bernadette of Lourdes said, "Mine is to inform, not convince." You must adopt this same attitude with your prodigal future friend of Saint Augustine. There are things you can do to prepare the soil of your prodigal's soul, and of your own, so that both can be more fruitful.

Surrender something as penance for your child. Your surrender may be your anger; it may be your sorrow. Offer it on the altar. Offer Masses or Rosaries or Holy Hours. Fast on Fridays or abstain from something, not because if you do certain things God will act, but because Jesus tells us to fast, to give alms, and to pray and that some things can be healed only by God. We simply help to prepare the souls of those we love by our sacrifices and surrenders. It is not easy. It would be much easier if God worked in a quid pro quo manner so that we would know, if our prayers weren't answered, that the fault was ours. It would be easier if we didn't have to allow for free will assenting to God's grace.

Therein lies the reason for our need to fast. Our struggles with surrendering little things reveal how easy it is to attach ourselves to the things of this world. Our desire to impose our wills should remind us that we remain in need of God's mercy, God's overwhelming offering of grace. History is replete with examples of lives in which, time after time after time, grace is offered and, time after time after time, it is refused. We are created, destined, and desired to live happily ever after. But we are free to either willingly seek such a reality or refuse God's offer of eternal friendship. Recognize that love is sacrifice, and be willing to let go of more than you plan, especially if your will protests, "I won't" or "I can't." Surrendering your will is a reminder, if nothing else, of how difficult it is to divorce the will from sin, from error, from appetite, from wants other than God, even when we know that He is the ultimate objective of life.

Having a child fallen away from the Church is the equivalent of a very long Lent. We are waiting for one who is dead to be alive again, for one who was lost to be found. We are constantly hoping that today will be the day—the day of resurrection, the Easter of our prodigal's soul. We are to present our entire lives as an example and trust God to do the rest. We wait in joyful hope each day for that day.

Hold On to the Nails, Not the Hurt

The ache of having an estranged prodigal isn't merely a sadness that comes and goes. It's the whole experience of brokenness. We have held our prodigal children in our arms, in our hearts, and they still live there — even when they've grown, even when they've rejected what we hoped would be their greatest treasure. It's hard not to feel as if we've failed in parenting, and those feelings can make it very difficult not to lose our temper, not to lash out. We will fail at times and say things that reveal our hurt.

Yesterday, a priest gave me a little treasure to hold in my heart. "When we hear another speak in anger," he told me, "it is their wounds speaking." I thought of students at my school who sometimes lash out, of relationships I cannot repair, and of those with whom, try as I might, I cannot bridge the gap between pain and love. When pain is speaking, we must, at the very least, seek to listen actively to the aches, the wounds. We should not aggravate these spiritual and emotional injuries, nor should we ignore them. We must be a salve if we're to cooperate with God in fostering the salvation of ourselves and of those we love.

We must also ensure that, when we do speak, it is not our own wounds doing the talking. Adoration is a good place to bring all the pains, to place them in the wounds of Christ, knowing that

He will heal all that needs healing. I can't recommend adoration enough. Learning to gaze at Jesus will help you learn how to gaze at your prodigal. And in being looked at with love by Jesus, you will learn to look at others as He does. Mary, too, gazed upon Jesus; she knew Him as no one else did. She held in her pain at the foot of the Cross, the pain of watching the One she loved crucified. That sort of supernatural strength and grace is a gift, found only by seeking truly to love, to love beyond the pain, beyond the hurt. So imitate Mary (boy, is this difficult for me), and share those aches with Jesus, but keep them in your heart. Cultivate a pondering heart like Mary's. God seeks to teach us to hold on to the nails, not the hurt, and He uses our moments of grief to pierce us with grace. Grief so pierced Mary's heart, so we can take comfort in knowing that she grieves with us.

Guard Your Heart,
so as to Remain Holy

Talking to others about your situation needs to be done with a healthy dose of prudence. Pray over whom to speak with about those closest to your heart.

Why? Because speaking of your pains to someone who is neither a counselor nor someone who loves your child creates three problems you cannot fix.

1. It presents your hurts as the defining component of your relationship with your child. It can overemphasize them in your own mind, predisposing you against your prodigal.

2. It creates a reputation of your loved one solely as a source of hurt, prejudicing others against him or her and reinforcing your hurts as well. Such conversations may become simply an outlet for your anger, which feeds itself and consumes love. We tend to report only the bad news because the good news is often not a story but a fleeting moment.

3. It may create new hurt if the people you speak to somehow disclose the information to your prodigal, even long after it has been said.

Saint Philip Neri understood the danger of talking about someone. To a woman who confessed the sin of gossip, he prescribed the penance of ripping feathers out of a pillow and letting them float down from the top of the church bell tower. He then told her to go into the town and collect all the feathers. She couldn't do it, and this was the point. What we say, we cannot unsay. Indiscreet words can injure long after they're said or written.

A counselor, your spouse, your spiritual adviser, your priest —these are examples of safe people to speak to about your pains, people with whom you already know your heart is safe. Grieve the brokenness with those who likewise know it and who know, above all, that you seek healing and resolution. But keep the list of those who have access to your heart's ache short because you don't want to fall into the habit of talking about someone, rather than loving him or her. As my mother wisely told me on occasion, "Guard your heart." The ones you love, they are your heart. You want them back because you love, and that means you hold them to have infinite dignity and worth, pearls of great price for which you would sell everything.

As a Parent, You Are
Never Finished Loving

When you first came home with a baby, you read books and subscribed to magazines. You consulted your parents, and there were support groups and helpful classes and loads of means of navigating the first few years of parenting. You gradually mastered the basics of telling when your baby needed to be fed, changed, picked up, put down, cleaned, played with, burped, and put to bed. You became an expert on potty training, on bedtime, on the basics of teaching how to dress, how to put away toys, count to ten, tie shoes, and the like.

When your child was ready to start school, again you were surrounded by veteran parents, teachers, lists of things to bring and to do, helpful articles in the paper and tips on the radio about easing the transition into that first day of school. There are similar support structures in place for entering high school, adjusting to adolescence, applying to college, and the like. There isn't, however, a helpful guide or support group for dealing with your child as an adult, and there certainly isn't a guide on your new role in his or her life. The thinking is that you've parented for eighteen years, so, by now, you should know what to do.

Adult sons and daughters will be in your life (God willing) much longer than they ever were as children. Your relationship will change several times as they and you move through the stages of life. Even if your children were fully invested in the Church, your role as Mom or Dad would change. You no longer act as chief provider and protector and presenter of all things true and beautiful, nor do you remain the center of your children's lives. Your new job is to pray, fast, provide an example by how you live, and offer encouragement when they show signs of maturation and self-sacrifice. Your new job is to become more and more someone they turn to, as we turn to Mary—someone who points in the direction of Christ and works as an intercessor. Like Mary, you are never finished because someone will always be "out of wine" (see John 2:1–11).

Lively Faith in Your Home Allows Divine Grace to Do Its Work

Stay steady in your faith in all things, but do not shut your children out of your life for not yet grasping who Jesus is and why you cling to Him so fiercely. Keep inviting them in through little things. Allow them to bump into your faith via your daily habits — prayers, feast days, the books you read. Your faith in practice carries grace to your children's hearts, perpetually putting Jesus in front of them, eroding the self-erected stones of philosophical, political, ideological, and social thinking they've substituted for the teachings of the Church.

This doesn't mean you shove it in their faces, but, by the same token, you should not feel unable to pray in your own home or to practice the Faith you know to be true, even if someone in the house does not. You should hold to your values and require that they be respected, as it is your home. If there are still children in formation in the house, you want to avoid confusion and should require at least quiet respect for what you hold in the home.

But follow Saint Monica and let them in, and let them see your joyous, fruitful, warm lives filled with the Holy Spirit. They may be moved by a younger child's first Confession or the sincerity of an older sibling's prayers. They may even opt to participate in some part of what you do. Each time they allow a little crack in the armor, God bursts in. Your job? Provide the opportunities for God to work by how you live.

How do you do this?

- Stay close to the sacraments, especially the Eucharist and Penance, so your life will be filled with the fruits of the Holy Spirit.
- Practice regular acts of penance and the spiritual and corporal acts of mercy, both organically (when an opportunity presents itself) and deliberately (by organizing opportunities yourself). Such a witness is compelling and more effective than any theological argument.
- Persist. Saint Monica set her heart and stayed the course. The fruit of her tears, fasting, and prayers was a son who is a saint and a Doctor of the Church.

We don't always get the luxury of a vision and a directive, a second Saint Monica story, giving us a gut check on our temptation to despair. We must remember how Saint Monica struggled at times with feeling that her efforts were fruitless. Seventeen years of tears is a long time. She kept after one local bishop to assist her in changing her son's mind and converting his heart. His first answer we've all heard if we've at some point gone to a priest about our wayward children: "Be patient" and "God's time will come." When Monica kept at it to the point of annoying the bishop (and I love this about Saint Monica), it provoked a response I find to be a great consolation both for her and all of us. "Go now, I beg you," he said. "It is not possible that the son of so many tears should perish."

Lord I Believe; Help My Unbelief (and Please, Please, Please Hurry Up!)

Once, while weeping and telling a priest about my situation, the priest gave me a sharp rebuke that cut me to the heart: "Your child is dead—spiritually speaking." My heart howled back, "Not dead but sleeping."

I knew that's how we're to see these prodigal children of ours. When we see a winter landscape, there are millions of seeds, waiting for spring. They appear dead, but they're not. They're sleeping. So pray for patience and forbearance. You'll certainly be given opportunities to practice both.

As a reminder to me of this moment, I often return to this story from the Gospel of Mark:

> When Jesus had crossed again in the boat to the other side, a great crowd gathered around him; and he was by the sea. Then one of the leaders of the synagogue named Jairus came and, when he saw him, fell at his feet and begged him repeatedly, "My little daughter is at the point of death. Come and lay your hands on her, so that she may be made well and live." So he went with him. (5:21–24)

Like Jairus, we must have faith to fall on our knees and ask Jesus to heal our child and make him or her live, and trust to ask repeatedly. The word used in the Scripture passage is "beg" because Jairus wants this with his whole heart. And he begs in front of a crowd because his heart so desires his daughter's healing that he is unashamed and because he trusts Jesus even before He acts on his daughter's behalf.

Another passage from Mark's Gospel that fits nicely with the story of Saint Monica is the passage concerning the woman suffering from a hemorrhage:

> She had endured much under many physicians and had spent all that she had, and she was no better, but rather grew worse. She had heard about Jesus and came up behind him in the crowd and touched his cloak, for she said, "If I but touch his clothes, I will be made well." Immediately her hemorrhage stopped; and she felt in her body that she was healed of her disease. Immediately aware that power had gone forth from him, Jesus turned about in the crowd and said, "Who touched my clothes?" And his disciples said to him, "You see the crowd pressing in on you; how can you say, 'Who touched me?'" He looked all around to see who had done it. But the woman, knowing what had happened to her, came in fear and trembling, fell down before him, and told him the whole truth. He said to her, "Daughter, your faith has made you well; go in peace and be healed of your disease." (5:26–34)

Our children may come up behind Jesus and seek secretly to be healed by Him. That's fine. Jesus is quite willing to let them come to Him through the back door, through the side window—anything. Whatever opening anyone gives in faith, Jesus walks through and breaks it wide open.

The story of Jairus continues:

> Some people came from the leader's house to say, "Your daughter is dead. Why trouble the teacher any further?" But overhearing what they said, Jesus said to the leader of the synagogue, "Do not fear, only believe." He allowed no one to follow him except Peter, James, and John, the brother of James. When they came to the house of the leader of the synagogue, he saw a commotion, people weeping and wailing loudly. When he had entered, he said to them, "Why do you make a commotion and weep? The child is not dead but sleeping." And they laughed at him. (5:35–40)

The world does not understand our sorrow, much less the idea that it could be cured. What I heard from the priest—"Your daughter is dead"—we also hear, in a sense, from others as we persist in worrying about our children's eternal salvation. The world says, "Your kid is an adult now, and it's his life. Don't worry about it. There's nothing you can do." This is true in one way but false in another. We cannot do anything about this situation. But the One we're petitioning? He can.

Mark writes next:

> Then He put them all outside and took the child's father and mother and those who were with him and went in where the child was. He took her by the hand and said to her, "*Talitha cum*," which means, "Little girl, get up!" And immediately the girl got up and began to walk about (she was twelve years of age). At this they were overcome

with amazement. He strictly ordered them that no one should know this and told them to give her something to eat. (5:40–43)

Oh, to have been in that house that day when Jesus said to give her something to eat. You can imagine how they prepared a feast like no other, for the one whom they loved had been lost and was found; was dead and now lives. Break out the fatted calf! We parents of fallen-away children live for the day when Jesus will take our children by the hand and tell them, "Get up!"

Here's one extra detail I love. It's not enough to have the miracle of the girl returning to life. Christ tells the parents to give her something to eat, for she needs ongoing nourishment. So, too, with our own prodigals; our job as people who love them is never over. We should always be feeding them and ourselves on the Faith.

Jesus can raise people from physical death, just as He can tell the paralyzed man, "Take up your mat and walk" (Mark 2:9). His power to forgive sins is all the greater, and thus we can feel confident that Jesus, the Son of God, the light of the world, can wake our sleeping brothers and sisters in Christ, our spouses, our parents, our children, our friends from their self-imposed stillness.

Be Brave, Even in Little Things

Sometimes the world demands that we not just quietly witness our Faith but that we publicly proclaim it. Right now, Catholics are having something of a "Peter moment," when it may seem easier to deny or to pretend the Faith isn't as important as it is. Is it the time to speak, or is it the time simply to serve?

There isn't one correct answer to this question, other than to love in everything you do and everything you say. In the Gospel, Jesus feeds the five thousand with two loaves and five fishes, and there are twelve baskets filled afterward with leftovers. He instructs the apostles to gather the fragments so that none will go to waste. It may be that you and your family are to bring the spiritual "fragments" from the Holy Mass back to your home so that those who chose not to attend the feast may yet be fed. Every meal, every interaction, is an opportunity to feed them. Christ asked Peter, "Simon, Son of John, do you love me?" When Peter says yes, Jesus commands him, "Feed my sheep" (John 21:17). If we love Christ, we must tend His sheep. We must lay down our lives for them.

How can we do this? Building up your relationship with your prodigal will, more often than not, involve the "little way" of witnessing, rather than the soaring, sword-like rhetoric of Saint Paul.

There are as many reasons why people leave the Church as there are people. It can be about a particular teaching of the Church they don't wish to follow, or a teaching of the Church that's not understood. It can be because the living examples they've encountered fell short. It can be because the living examples didn't explain why they do what they do. It can be because they feel vulnerable. It can be because they don't "feel" the presence of Christ in the Church or don't believe they have or can have a true relationship with God.

Becoming a faithful follower of Christ means falling in love. Given the myriad of reasons why a person might fall away from the Faith, it becomes the lover's job to provide reasons (without arguing) why one might fall in love with Christ. Your witness in the home must illustrate your love for Christ through the love and care you show toward the person in your family who does not know Christ. Let your family meals bring a sense of beauty, peace, and joy to your household, and let that be your means of gradual, increasing witness.

Feed the Lord's sheep as Peter did, and trust that Christ will become known to them, perhaps only in the ordinary breaking of bread at home. Revealing Christ with your charitable words, with food and laughter, shared memories and plans for future events/tasks—these are little but greatly courageous things to do. This slow, steady offering, manifested in little things done with great love will win hearts. Our job, again, as a lover of both God and the prodigal, is to trust that God will turn all of our efforts to grace and reveal to our prodigals the true peace and joy to be found in His Church.

Jesus Gives Lavishly, More Than We Can Even Ask

The Scripture stories we examined from Mark's Gospel reveal much about our situation with our adult children. We need to recognize that we ourselves are in both stories. We are both the wounded and the one asking for another to be healed. We are hoping to touch the hem of Jesus' garment and have our problem cease. But we are also like the synagogue official, coming to ask Jesus for help on behalf of the one we love. In both stories, we are coming to Jesus for help, and the very act of seeking Him is an illustration of our faith. Our faith is what Jesus wants of us; it is what He thirsts for.

A priest I follow talked about the questions Jesus asks when people approach Him. "What is it you want?"—Jesus knows what we need, but we must articulate it. "Do you want me to heal you?"—Christ desires to heal us but respects our freedom to refuse. He works through and with our faith but will never impose His will on our souls, and the same holds true for those we love who do not adhere to the Faith. Christ acts around us, through others, and courts our souls, but He will not enter into our hearts unless we allow it.

I take great comfort in the lavish generosity Christ shows in His miracles. He heals all ten lepers, He feeds the five thousand, and He creates six large vats of the best wine. He helps the apostles catch so many fish that their nets almost burst. He heals those who approach, those who ask. Sometimes they cry out, "Jesus, Son of David, have pity on me," even when others tell them to be quiet (see Mark 10:48). It's never inappropriate to ask Jesus to have pity on your heart or to ask the Divine Physician to heal the one you love. It's never wrong to ask even when others think otherwise.

Our prodigals are like the paralyzed man, carried by four of his friends who break open the roof to get him to Jesus (Mark 2:3–4). They are also like the man sitting beside the pool at Bethzatha, unable to move, having suffered for thirty-eight years in that condition. Jesus asks him, "Do you wish to get well?" and the sick man answers, "I have no one to put me in the pool when the water is stirred up" (John 5:6–7). No one was helping the man get to the pool to be healed. We can help carry our loved ones to Jesus by praying, but we should also remember that Jesus will come to them in His own time, if they wish to get well.

Either way, we need to ask God to pour His grace out upon our lost children. He is the only one with the capacity to transform their hearts. Again, the Gospel gives us great confidence in the power of intercessory prayer. When the Roman centurion asks Jesus to heal his servant, Jesus answers, "I will come." But the "centurion answered, 'Lord, I am not worthy to have you come under my roof. But only say the word, and my servant will be healed. For I, too, am a man under authority, with soldiers under me. I tell one to go, and he goes; and another to come, and he comes. I tell my servant to do something, and he does it'" (Matt. 8:5–9). So it is with Jesus. His word makes water into wine, forgives sins, raises people from the dead, and calls all of us to Him. Let us learn to pray, "Lord, I am not worthy to have You under my roof, but only say the word and Your servant will be healed." We cannot merit a miracle. We cannot merit God's grace. We can only ask, receive, and celebrate when we perceive God acting in our lives.

The Rosary Is Your Best Tool

You knew we'd talk about the Rosary eventually.

There's not a better tool for helping to orient one's own spirit when dealing with others who, for whatever reason, have rejected the Church. Ask the Blessed Mother to knit your hearts together; ask her to mold your heart so you can respond to your child with great charity. With each Hail Mary, meditate on Mary's virtues—obedience, humility, docility, charity, generosity, patience, forbearance, gentleness, reverence, and kindness—and ask that they be increased in you. In the next decade, ask for these same gifts of the Holy Spirit for your child—wisdom, understanding, fear of the Lord, counsel, fortitude, knowledge, piety—whatever it is you see as a hurdle in your child's life. Ask for your child's friends, ask for your spouse, for all affected by the loss of whichever one you love who is not at Christ's table. Ask Mary to tap that child on the shoulder, to show that child her Son. Ask on each bead, and when you run out of petitions, say "Thank you" on all the remaining beads.

When meditating on the Mysteries of the Rosary, imagine placing your child on the altar with Mary when she presents Jesus in the Temple. Imagine finding your child with Jesus in the Temple. Ask Saint John the Baptist to help rekindle in your child's heart knowledge of his or her baptismal gifts. If your prodigal is married, ask Mary to ask Jesus to turn the water of his or her marriage into wine. If your prodigal is angry at you, be meek, be gentle, and practice the Beatitudes. Hope for the day of your child's return, as the Blessed Mother hoped for the Resurrection. She knows your heart is pierced. She knows the sorrow you feel, and she wants to bring you consolations and to help lead your child back to her Son. Pray the Rosary, and she will hold your hand throughout this journey.

There isn't a single mystery explored in the Rosary—Joyful, Sorrowful, Glorious, or Luminous—that we can delve into without finding a connection to our own stories and struggles in family life. If you want your loved one to return to Jesus, pray the Rosary. Pray it daily. It isn't that you have to pray so many Rosaries to get God to do what you want, but in continually meditating on the mysteries of the life of Christ, you'll come to know more of God's love and become more like His most perfect disciple, Mary.

The more we become manifestations of God's love to others, the more likely it is that that love will pierce our children's hearts and lead them back to Christ. The Rosary remains (as affirmed by many a saint) a singularly effective means of uniting our hearts to God's heart, which draws all men to itself. To the extent that we manifest God's love, we will be attractive, luminous witnesses to our prodigals, drawing them to God and allowing Him to work on even more hearts than the ones we hold up in petition.

Find Your Consolation in Christ, and Hold Fast to the Gospel

There are great consolations for us as we endure the disconnect in our hearts when someone in our family is estranged from the Faith. We have our suffering Savior, rejected in all acts of sin, and we have the company of all the saints who likewise weathered trials among their friends and family, suffering greatly while on Earth. They are praying for us, and they work for the triumph of each of us. It's easier to hold on when we know we're not alone.

When conflict with your prodigal arises (and it will), not fighting gets hard and the temptation is to throw verbal and emotional punches. When we fight, we are like the apostle cutting off the ear of the slave (Luke 22:49–51). Aggression is not the means by which to save or defend Jesus or even ourselves. Put away the "sword," and remember the reality of being a disciple of Jesus.

Still, as the years roll by, and the conflict continues, it's tempting to flee— either to wash your hands like Pilate, because the person you love has made his or her choice, or to opt for the equally empty "All Dogs Go to Heaven" theory, in which everyone gets a free pass on about all that he thinks, does, and says, so long as he's not an ax murderer or Hitler.

The gospels of compartmentalization and relativism, like the gospels of prosperity and of merit-earned-heaven, are heresies that reveal a person's desire to control or manipulate God and one another. God's love is a given, not something we earn. God's mercy is an offering we must receive. God's grace is there for the poor and the rich, for the just and the unjust; it is like the sun, which shines on all alike. God offers us all forgiveness for our sins.

His is not a gospel that professes that there is nothing to forgive, that there is no sin. It is likewise not a gospel that allows those who follow the Faith to lord it over their prodigal siblings, to feel entitled to more of God's grace. The saints understood that they were in constant need of God's grace, and the more they received, the more they knew they needed God's mercy. We can't quite grasp such humility because these people who do holy, heroic things don't seem to need to be humble. But the more aware we are of our own failure to live the true Gospel message, the more merciful we shall become and the less likely we will be to spend any energy condemning anyone else. The Gospel is hard, because it requires us to love, and love is always based on sacrifice. But the Gospel also promises that if you follow Jesus, if you trust in Him, you will know abundant joy. So remember that you're beloved, and so, too, is your prodigal, and hold fast to the Gospel.

Christ is with you in this suffering. Your agony is His Agony in the Garden. Your wincing at unkind words, cruel accusations, and arguments is likewise His scourging. Your frustration at all the errors and corrosive ideologies that prick your heart is His crown of thorns. Christ walks with us, Christ carries our cross, Christ submits to death on the Cross to win our children back. He has shed every last drop of His blood to win back each and every soul as if it were the only soul to win.

This struggle with a person who does not follow the Faith or, in some cases, does not even acknowledge love, is without a set ending. It is an open wound. We grow used to weathering it without wearying. If we can learn not to let it scar over but to let it be a means of entering more deeply into our Faith and into Christ's heart, it can be for us like the open wounds of Christ —fully healed, yet not closed.

Watch Yourself

When we long for someone to return to the Faith, there's a danger of spiritual pride. We know our Faith to be true, and we are practicing it to the best of our ability. That knowledge can easily be warped into pride. We may scoff at the Pharisee praying, "Lord, I thank you that I'm not like that poor sinner." But if we're not deeply aware of our own flaws, the Pharisee's attitude and our own may become dangerously similar.

Be still and know that He is there. Jesus is in the storm with you. In all conflicts, one either fights or flees. For those who feel the desire to fight, a reminder: no one is won to Christ by war. This is not a court battle, and you are not the lawyer arguing the case, much as you might wish. It is not your task to engage in tit-for-tat apologetics with this person, but to love him or her.

The phrase "Jesus, I trust in You," painted in the portrait of Divine Mercy, is not merely a pretty sentiment. It is a strong proclamation of faith—rather like "love your enemies," which sounds lovely until you have to live it. For those who struggle with wanting to wash their hands of the conflict and quit, a reminder: we are not disinterested bystanders in this struggle. We are friends, spouses, parents, children. We are also all brothers and sisters in Christ, whose mission is to bring all those we love to the Church. We must ride out this storm in the boat with Jesus, trusting Him.

On a practical note, as mentioned earlier, if you have a prodigal who raises serious objections to the Church, ask him to write out his objections in detail. Writing will clarify what he professes and why he professes it. It will also allow for a discussion of ideas if you, too, reply in writing. It worked for Saint Paul and Saint Augustine. You can even address your prodigal's concerns with writings from the saints and Doctors of the Church. Turning the battles into dialogues is the goal, not so that you can win the argument (you may not, either because of unwillingness to hear or because the other person's problem can't be solved through an argument) but so that your prodigal's curiosity may be sparked and grow. This cannot happen if no exploration of ideas is allowed.

The Bishop of the Abandoned Tabernacle, Saint Manuel González García, spoke of encountering a church in which the tabernacle was covered with cobwebs, droppings, and assorted debris. It lay abandoned, with bits of a molding consecrated Host left unvenerated. His first thought was to flee, until he heard in his heart, "Must you, too, abandon me?" These children, these people we love who do not follow the Faith, have abandoned the tabernacle. Will we, too, abandon Christ in them by washing our hands of the matter?

The white martyrdom of everyday life, the surrendering of minutia, and the willful enduring and embracing of a cross made of a million splinters is a heroic feat for which we will receive a martyr's reward if we conform our hearts and minds to God's will. It's not easy; it's almost unheard of in this day and age, but it is this redemptive suffering that gives meaning to the pain we experience because someone we love no longer recognizes the God who is love or doesn't practice the Faith we've pointed to as the most whole means by which we can obtain happiness and abundant life.

Our pride may show itself by overt displays of piety or by how we speak of our prodigals when they are not present. Our anger may metastasize into resentment, into passive-aggressive actions, gossip, dismissive phrases, despair, or petty barbs. It's hard not to take a child's decision to leave the Faith as a critique of our parenting. It's hard not to want to strike back, to fight, or to shame the child in some way or guilt him or her into returning. This is why we need to follow Mary and Joseph's example. Mary "kept all these things in her heart," which we know was pierced (see Luke 2:35, 51). Joseph, likewise, speaks volumes about his deep love by his obedience and silence in the Gospels. Isaiah 50:4, "The Lord has given me a well-trained tongue," should be our goal. Saint James warns us, in chapter 3, of the tremendous damage a careless word can do, likening our words to a small fire that can set a whole forest ablaze. So we should pray for this gift of tempered speech. "If anyone does not fall short in speech, he is a perfect man, able to bridle his whole body also."

While it was once our job to manage our children's lives and to teach them the Faith, it remains our job now to witness humbly and to let God use us in their lives. We are conduits and conveyors of God's love, not the enforcers of God's law. Ergo, our prayers should be both, "Lord, be merciful to me, a sinner" and, "Father, forgive them; for they know not what they do" (see Luke 18:13; 23:34). We are to petition for them and ourselves, knowing that God loves each of us beyond what we can even know. Our whole job as parents now is to pray for our children, for mercy for ourselves and the whole world. It's not a "washing of the hands" to say this. Rather, if we can't, by constantly loving our children, get them to hear what we say, or live it, or agree with it, we can be always about the business of washing their feet.

Sacraments and Sacramentals

At Mass one Sunday, I found myself thrown into sorrow, thinking about the rejection of the Faith within my family. The Holy Spirit heard my cry, and the priest talked about God's love and grace being like water in the desert. Water is necessary for us to be alive. It's necessary, it refreshes, it restores, it revives.

The priest spoke of the sacrament of Reconciliation being like water for our parched souls. He also mentioned that water erodes all things, even rock, and the psalm we heard that day said, "If today you hear His voice, harden not your hearts" and spoke of breaking hearts of stone. The Old Testament, too, spoke of Moses striking the rock, from which water flowed to restore and nurture the Israelites. Christ's heart is pierced on the Cross, and blood and water flow forth, restoring us to God's grace. All of it fit, and the knowledge of this reality, of God wearing down rocky hearts with love, made me cry.

My other kids wondered why their mother was breaking down just before Holy Communion, but it was too overwhelming for me. All I could do was hold on to the image of water breaking forth through the rock, knowing, one day, that that could be my child's heart. If I felt this much joy over the mere thought of my dear one returning to the Church, how much more does God rejoice? How much more does God want it? And how much more will God do than my little prayers and petitions and slivers of sufferings offered up to win back the hearts of those He made for love alone?

If we still aren't sure how much God longs for their return, look at this prayer attributed to Jesus speaking to Saint Teresa of Calcutta. Read it first to your own soul. Then insert your child's name and reread it, and know that it is always true:

> It is true. I stand at the door of your heart, day and night. Even when you are not listening, even when you doubt it could be me, I am there, waiting for even the smallest signal of your response, even the smallest suggestion of an invitation that will permit me to enter.
>
> I want you to know that each time you invite me, I do come always, without fail. Silent and invisible I come, yet with a power and a love most infinite, bringing the many gifts of my Spirit. I come with my mercy, with my desire to forgive and heal you, with a love for you that goes beyond your comprehension.
>
> A love in each detail, so grand like the love I have received from my Father. 'I have loved all of you as the Father has loved me'" (John 15:10).

As the prayer continues, the fullness of Christ's love for each of our souls is expressed in the words, "I thirst." He groans in longing for our love.

It's hard not to weep at how much more God loves us than we can imagine. It's also comforting to know that our own manifestations of love are nowhere close to God's. We can only imitate or echo His declaration "I thirst." Know that Jesus feels your agony over your child's being not in full communion with Him. It is His agony you share, because you both love this soul. He thirsts for your prodigal as He thirsts for you.

It's Still Hard and Will Be Until It Isn't

No matter what we do, it is not easy to have a loved one who has fallen away from the faith. The passage of time allows you to keep going, but the ache remains and reopens, particularly around holidays and high feast times such as Christmas or Easter, at weddings, and even on secular holidays, such as Mother's Day. The temptation to quit, rage, rant, cry, or lash out will be ever present in those special moments, when what divides us is front and center.

Contemplating the Blessed Mother (who "kept all these things in her heart"), we need to fold all that pain into our hearts, to accept these wounds as being like Christ's in His hands, feet, and side. It's comforting to know that the Blessed Mother will walk with us. She'll hold on to us, even as she tries to lead those we love back to her Son. She will, through her example, help us to connect with these people we love so much. One of Mary's titles is "Undoer of Knots," and we need her to undo our anger, our disappointment, our frustration, our fatigue. We need her to undo our pain and our need to have our efforts, past and present, validated. Even better, being our Mother, she knows what we need.

So ask. Ask her to infuse your heart with her humility. Ask her to mold your heart to be patient. Ask her to help you be quiet when you should be quiet, to speak when you should speak, and to offer everything at the altar for Christ. Praying the Rosary will help you, as it gives you an offering you can make daily on your family member's behalf. Stay close to Mary, and trust that she'll feed your soul, even as you hope, by your petitions to Heaven, to help your prodigal find his or her way back to the Father's house.

Remember, it will still be hard. Jesus tells us that if we follow Him, we must embrace the cross. This suffering is a cross. It is heavy. It has splinters. We didn't want it. We will be laughed at for feeling it deeply. We will be told just to drop it. It will feel as if there are few who understand. There will be some who weep with us, some who wipe our faces, and some who carry it with us. But the most important thing is the one who is carrying it before us, with whom we are participating in the redemption of the world, if we allow our pain to be so used. Jesus is with us in every agony, every scourge, every splinter, every insult, every hurt, in all the rage, in all of it. Jesus is with us; He is holding the cross tighter than we are. Jesus is carrying it. We are carrying it with Him, the way a toddler helps with bringing in the groceries. We are simply offering our widow's mite because it is all we can do. And that is all God asks of us.

But it will still sometimes be very hard.

The Domestic Church Is Your Refuge

Part of weathering this long wandering in the desert is holding on to the rest of your family, leading all of them through the same journey. You will need to discover the spiritual gifts of your spouse, your other children, your extended family, and your friends. You will need them to pray with and for you. You will need them to listen and to talk. You will need them to help, not to fill the hole left by the one who isn't at Mass, but to build up all the rest of the Body of Christ while you trust in Jesus to do the real healing. You will need to spend time on the rest of your life, on doing ordinary things, infused with your faith. You will need to shore up the foundations of your domestic church by being (despite any pain and sufferings caused by the one estranged) a joyful witness to what the family is supposed to be—an outward sign of the eternal reality of the Trinity, a passionate, infinite exchange of love.

You are evangelizing your child, and that's best done by being infectious with your joy. Don't be an infomercial for the good life. Witnessing is not a "Hey, we're having a great time; come join us!" kind of hard sell. It is a whisper. It is an invitation. When your prodigal allows himself or herself to be part of the family, to participate, fold that child into it with as much ordinary affection as the situation allows. You're not a super-zealous cheerleader for the Faith. You're this child's parent, and this is the domestic church. The hallmarks of the family should be peace, comfort, warmth, kindness, gentleness, patience, and good humor. That's a long list of virtues to flavor every moment, and it won't always be possible, but with grace and willful prayer and participation, it will become the norm. Build your domestic church on strong foundations, and storms will not destroy it.

At Best, We're Junior Assistants

I joke with my friends about parenting: "We're not in control; we're just the ones responsible." It's true that we are not in command of our lives, and as anyone who deals with adult or teen prodigals knows, we're nowhere near in control of anyone else's soul. Our whole job is and always has been preparation. We are always the sous chefs in this endeavor. We prepare and propose. Jesus does the work.

We have to hope that, somehow, we can help prepare the soil for the seed, and we must keep doing so each day of our lives. No one likes to think of the seed not being received, but Jesus doubles down on the reality of our free will in the familiar Parable of the Sower:

> Hear then the parable of the sower. When any one hears the word of the kingdom and does not understand it, the evil one comes and snatches away what is sown in his heart; this is what was sown along the path. As for what was sown on rocky ground, this is he who hears the word and immediately receives it with joy; yet he has no root in himself, but endures for a while, and when tribulation or persecution arises on account of the word, immediately

he falls away. As for what was sown among thorns, this is he who hears the word, but the cares of the world and the delight in riches choke the word, and it proves unfruitful. As for what was sown on good soil, this is he who hears the word and understands it; he indeed bears fruit, and yields, in one case a hundredfold, in another sixty, and in another thirty. (Matt. 13:18–23, RSVCE)

Remember, our whole job is to prepare the soil. We are neither the sower nor the seed, but merely the hands that till the ground, move around the dirt, and occasionally water and add fertilizer. God's doing the work; we're trying to be His hands and feet and cooperate with His grace, trusting Him to bring about the miracle, despite the messes we make of our lives when we try to take over.

Recognize Your Weak Points

Everyone who eliminates God from his life finds a substitute. The most common substitutes are power, wealth, and fame, but there are many others. When we have a child who is far away from the Faith, it helps to consider what his or her substitute might be — not because we can then say, "Aha!" and take away the temptation, but because we can then, at the very least, help to cultivate the corresponding virtue.

Examining the weeds and thorns that choke off the good seed, we may find that materialism and the desire for wealth don't always mean caviar dreams and champagne wishes. Sometimes, these weeds materialize as a desire for security, for comfort, which enables sloth in the spiritual realm. Sometimes, the thorns that choke off faith life come from working to the point of becoming a slave to success. Sometimes, the thorns keep one so entertained, so distracted, so stimulated, they don't allow the quiet necessary to hear God's gentle, small voice, let alone to be open to anything beyond the five senses and the next moment. A person can become consumed by consumerism, even if he doesn't sport a six-figure income. The desire to have, to acquire, and to feel secure and comfortable in all things is a desire to rest in something other than God. It is a desire to be spiritually dead, to shut out God. A well-lived life, on the other hand, involves always encountering others and making the choice to love and sacrifice at every opportunity.

The cure for the weeds and thorns is spiritual pruning. Fasting is a great way to start weeding out the excess that we thought was necessary. It isn't just a "Well, I'll give up chocolate," kind of activity. Instead, begin by praying over whether this is what God wants you to do, and, if so, how. Pray, "Am I called to fast for this person? If so, what am I to let go of?"

If, after prayer, you do decide to take on such a sacrifice, you should then prepare yourself for fasting. Go to Confession to free yourself from sin. Receive Holy Communion, your daily bread, and write down what you are doing, for whom you are doing it, why you are doing it, and for how long. This will help to keep you accountable to yourself, to help conform your heart, mind, and will with God's. Place the note under a crucifix or a rosary, depending on the method of prayer you will use in conjunction with the fasting, and look at it often. Hold the note while you pray.

If this seems too physical, remember that all the sacraments are outward, physical signs of the invisible reality of God's grace working in us. Holding on to the promise we've made, as we've promised to pray, and surrendering whatever we've chosen to give up is how we should attempt to fast successfully. Letting go of something we take pleasure in reminds us of how difficult it is to detach ourselves from the desire to be sated, to be full of something. It reminds us that we are, at all times, empty in some capacity because we do not have full communion with God. It humbles us so that we can recognize — we who know God is worthy of all our love — that we are still slaves to sin until we learn to cooperate fully with divine grace.

Walking with Them

Showing a concern for your prodigal's happiness and well-being and acknowledging the good values he or she already holds is a quiet form of evangelization. Think of Ruth: "Wherever you go, let me go, too" (see Ruth 1:16). If the person is open to personal change with respect to certain behavior, even if he or she is not willing to address the issue from a spiritual standpoint, walk with your prodigal and help facilitate the change. For example, if your loved one has a problem with food, prepare meals together or exercise together. Be a companion, because having someone to walk with him or her can make all the difference.

Just as children prune away the selfishness of the parents, as the mother and father must put aside some of their own desires to serve their children, so also serving a prodigal means pruning oneself. As you try to help the one you love who is far from the Faith, you must make sure your own soul isn't being choked by desires for glory, honor, power, or, specifically, the esteem of others for seeking to help another to find God. By frequent Confession and Communion and by steeping yourself in the Scriptures, the seed of faith planted in your heart can grow deeper.

An examination of conscience at the beginning and end of each day might help you to recognize weaknesses and patterns of behavior that may counteract your attempts to evangelize. You must learn to recognize the weeds as they grow and root them out whenever and wherever they sprout. Having good truth-teller friends or a spiritual adviser helps. None of us arrives at Heaven's gate without the love and encouragement of another.

Telling your prodigal about your own struggles and wrestling with God might also help reveal to that person that no one this side of the veil is fully settled in his faith and that people of faith do continue to ask questions and to struggle and must choose to love over their own impulses to indulge. Who knows? The prodigal in your life might be the one to point out weeds you don't wish to see, and thus both of you can walk together toward Christ.

Love Will Break Hearts of Stone

Rocky soil of the heart is harder to deal with than weeds. The gardener who seeks to sow good seed on bad earth must churn the soil, digging up and removing the rocks. The swiftest way of softening the soil of one's heart is by serving the suffering. As the parent of a prodigal, finding moments when you can show empathy and be of service to others who suffer becomes part of the process of walking with them. It requires willful seeking and willful serving. Praying for a tender heart — for the desire to cultivate such hearts in others — is a good way of asking God to give you the grace to weather the special circumstances you've been given.

You will also be required to act as an ambassador of hope for your child when he or she encounters suffering. The hardest thing for any person of goodwill to understand on Earth is that God allows suffering. You have to show your prodigal how to see God in the little things and how to bring God into those moments that otherwise would be unbearable.

You have to hope, each time you do this, that this time your prodigal will encounter Christ in His distressing disguise. That doesn't mean you need to schedule a trip to the soup kitchen each Saturday, although it might be a good idea. But you certainly need to ask the Holy Spirit to guide you on how best to serve and ask Him to provide opportunities for you and those you love, including your prodigal, to practice mercy toward others. You cannot force anything, but you can let God work through and with you, trusting that in His time, He will. (Side note: all time is God's time; it just isn't always being used as you or I would want.) Sometimes, the rocks being broken into pieces are our own.

Become familiar with the works of mercy, both spiritual and corporal, and determine how to begin practicing them in your everyday life. Here's a reminder of what they are, in case you've forgotten. The seven corporal (meaning "bodily") acts of mercy are to feed the hungry, to give drink to the thirsty, to clothe the naked, to shelter the homeless, to visit the sick, to visit the imprisoned, and to bury the dead. The seven spiritual acts of mercy are to instruct the ignorant, to counsel the doubtful, to admonish the sinner, to bear wrongs patiently, to forgive offenses willingly, to comfort the afflicted, and to pray for the living and the dead.

None of these works are done in isolation from the others. They are all knit together in Christ's words, "Whatever you do to the least of my brothers, you do unto me" and "Love your neighbor as yourself" (see Matt. 25:40; 19:19). Prayerfully discern how to go about this in your own life, and, again, consent to be used by God for others. It is the surest way to break up the rocks in your soul and provide opportunities for God to do the real work.

The Soul Stolen Away

The idea of the good seed being carried off feels more dramatic and aggressive than the more natural occurrence of rocky soil or weeds. And it's supposed to. The birds represent the evil one, seeking to prevent anything from taking root. Modern sensibilities chafe at the idea that God is invested in our lives yet seemingly does not prevent evil, such as the apparent theft of God's own word from souls. When someone we love leaves the Faith willfully and, in some cases, with an added dose of hostility, however, it does feel as if the person we knew has somehow been stolen.

We deeply feel our loved ones' absence in the pew during Mass, and we notice if they are not with us at special occasions, because we love them and want them present in our lives, both now and in the infinity to come.

The devil wants no one to make it to Heaven, not one of us. If by stealing one, he can cause the rest of us to abandon God in despair, he's gotten quite a deal. So he puts distractions in the way of each of us, especially in the way of the one who might be tempted to "go back to his Father's house." And it's an easy trap for parents to start to resent a prodigal adult child or to want to use power to rein the child in.

Jesus, however, does not want the birds to take away the seed. He sows new seed each day and stands at the doors of our hearts and knocks. The birds carry away any seed we do not allow to sink into our hearts. If nothing else, pray for Jesus to keep working our soil until there are no weeds or rocks, until each of us is ready to receive more deeply.

The battle for souls is not won by us but by Christ, and He awaits our participation and cooperation. We also know that God causes whoever consents to yield ten-, twenty-, fifty-, a hundredfold. All He requires from each of us is that our faith be planted deeply. So pray for your faith and that of your children, that the soil of their souls may be tilled and their faith may be planted deeply by Christ. Trust that He will come again each day to sow more seed, to give us ample opportunities in the hope that, before the moment of our death, our souls will say, "Let it be done to me according to your will."

How Can We Be at Peace if One We Love Is Lost?

It's frightening to know that someone we love dearly is far from home. It should be. It brings up a question. How can we know joy if one we love is lost? Having a child estranged from the Faith gives us a glimpse of Christ's Agony in the Garden. If Christ wept blood for the souls who would refuse Him, and He's God, it is no wonder that we weep. We don't know what will happen in the end. We don't know who will make it into Heaven (other than the saints), who resides in Hell, or who is in Purgatory.

Christ came so that we might have abundant life. God wills for us to be with Him in Heaven, but that can happen only if our wills are to will God's will. We may struggle to comply with God's will in our thoughts and actions, even when we theoretically want to obey His will. Nevertheless, we should rejoice in God's great mercy, rather than cower in fear. God wills our good because He is love.

We can take great comfort in knowing that each day offers new opportunities to "begin again" and try somehow to be more loving toward our prodigals, for whom we may be the only face of God they will ever encounter. Jesus comes to the woman at the well, tells her of all the things she has done, and still He offers her living water. He's always offering Himself to each of us, and He's always telling us, "I know all you've done, and, yes, I still offer you everything. I have shed my blood to win you back, for you are the pearl of great price." God the Father tells us, "I give you everything again today to show you how much you are loved." And He sends forth the Holy Spirit to help us and all those around us, bringing each of us closer to Him.

We have one option if we would will God's will. We should intentionally offer our prayers, pain, sufferings, sacrifices, fasting, and service—all of it as a gift on the altar in thanksgiving for God's goodness, in praise of His mercy, and in delight at His great love.

Over and over again, tell yourself that God loves your prodigal even more than you do, and He is working on it with you and through you. Tell yourself also that God loves you more than you love yourself and is using this trial to bring you into deeper communion with Him. God will send forth His Spirit, and our offerings will be transformed into even greater grace. To present our trials as gifts and to accept them as opportunities for prayer is not easy to do, because it requires practice on our part. It also requires trust in Divine Providence, trust that God is acting, that God will continue to act, and that He will order all these things to the good of each of us.

Taking Up the Cross

Sometimes, we can hear God's word and almost fall apart at the beauty of it—until we have to live it. Loving your enemy, forgiving your brother seventy times seven, being your brother's keeper, taking up your cross? Taking and eating His Body and drinking His Blood? All of it sounds crazy. All of it sounds very difficult. All of it sounds impossible without grace. And it is!

The fallen part of each of us rails against God and our neighbor. The fallen part rails against the ingratitude of our children in not holding the Faith. We raised them. We taught them. They should be like us. They should value what we value.

Didn't we show them? Didn't we teach them? Why have they left? Why can't it be easy? Go to Church! Stay in school! Don't have sex! Don't abuse your body, mind, heart, or soul! It would be so much simpler if we all just followed the rules. Why can't they? Why didn't they? Eventually, we turn back to complaining to God: if you want all of us and love us more than we can ever love each other, why isn't it easier?

We all suffer from Original Sin and all the sins we commit. We want it to be easy. But it isn't. We'd like to be able to bring our children back by saying the right prayers, checking off the right boxes, or by their merely agreeing to go along and follow all the rules. But none of that works, not for us, not for them, not for Christ. Taking up the cross means just that—taking up a cross, being willing to suffer and suffering well for someone else. Christ's love is immeasurable but it is illustrated by the extension of His hands and His feet on the Cross. Our love is illustrated by the extent to which we're willing to lay down our lives like Christ.

People rail against God and the Church and the Faith for the same reason we ourselves fail God and the Church and the Faith. We have not yet subjugated ourselves to the point of death on a cross. We are not yet saints. We are not yet humble enough to know our place in the universe as someone loved by the one who made the universe. If we who love God, who follow the Faith, who profess to be part of the Church, do not yet know how to kneel before our Lord, we should be patient with those who do not yet know what we know and love the God we love.

Christ didn't call us to be part of an elite group of Pharisees. He didn't call us to check off the boxes. He calls each of us, including the prodigals in our lives, to a radical friendship with Him. That's done on a day-by-day, moment-by-moment basis through sacrifice, sublimation, service, and prayer. It's done by surrendering. It's done by listening, by becoming steeped ever more in the mystery of God through the sacraments, through Scripture, through the writings of the saints, through service, and through sacred tradition. God is a tireless wooer of our souls, and He'll use argument, beauty, suffering, success—whatever it takes—to win us.

Being Honest

All of this discussion is about the one thing that preoccupies anyone who loves someone who is far from the Faith. How do we maintain or grow an honest relationship with the person we love when faith is such an intrinsic part of who we are?

There are temptations to avoid discussing religion, which gives a false sense of security because of the constant silence. Agreeing to a "cold war" in which nothing ever gets examined and everyone just tries to avoid the emotional land mines is not peace. It's tension until an explosion happens.

It's not peace, it's not quiet, and it is the opposite of a family.

Families don't simply tolerate differences. Families love all their members. Love isn't tolerance; it's service. It's mercy. It's warmth. It's welcoming. It's sacrificial. Families love. Families forgive. Families hold together.

This doesn't mean you drag out the fights. It simply means you look for common ground and common values to build upon, wherever they might be. You look to play together. You look to feast together. You look to work together on things that matter to the whole family. You seek opportunities to build upon all that you can touch, taste, feel, see, and hear in order to knit your hearts together, whether it's watching hockey or raking leaves or cooking fried chicken. If you're not sure where to find such opportunities, ask the Holy Spirit to guide you, and listen to the concerns, desires, and dreams of your prodigal.

Look at the life of Christ for inspiration. He went to the markets. He ate with sinners. He visited the homes of those ignored and rejected by others. He spent time with whomever He encountered. Spend time. That is one gift we can always offer. Being present does not mean inaction. People often think of Saint Martha being busy and Saint Mary, her sister, being still. Saint Mary was not still. She was fully present to the person of Jesus. Be still in yourself and fully present to your prodigal, and you will find you have more capacity to love and engage that person.

Your Prodigal and the Rest of Your Family

Do the ordinary things, but invite your prodigal to join in where you can and where it's appropriate. If you have younger children who see this rejection of the Faith, and you're fearful of the older sibling setting a bad example, it's an opportunity for you, too, to be an example — an example of God the Father's perpetual, lavish love. It's an opportunity to remind the younger child to pray for his or her sibling. It's also an opportunity to talk about free will and about what you hope for each of your children: that each will know and love the Faith, but that it's a process. Not everyone gets to where we would hope at the same time.

Raising children in the Faith isn't brainwashing, and it isn't demanding unthinking obedient responses to a collection of rules. It's introducing those we love to the One who is love and teaching them that all we do is a manifestation either of our love for God and each other or of our desire to follow our own wills instead. It's an opportunity to teach them that God can be known in creation, in prayer, in the Bible, in others, in service, and, most importantly and intimately, in the sacraments.

Your children can learn the unique specialness of their Faith and why it matters, even as you explain that not everyone always understands or internalizes this knowledge. They can learn to see that God is always speaking in the whispers of our lives, inviting us to love. They can come to know that loving someone who believes differently or struggles with the Faith is loving as God loves. They can learn that following the Faith involves sacrifice, struggle, and willingness to serve, even as they learn that loving a sibling can demand the same thing.

The Dangers of Engaging in Intellectual Combat

There's a desire to win, to defeat your prodigal with apologetics, with the lives of the saints, or with moral reasoning. It's understandable. We wouldn't hold to a Faith we didn't believe to be true. And having someone you love dismiss or reject what you know to be true damages your capacity to witness to other members of your family who are still in faith formation. It makes everything more difficult. We know we're supposed to correct errors in thinking, so doesn't this apply in a particular way when dealing with family?

But winning the argument with your prodigal may mean losing the war. In this war, it is the soul that must be won, and anything other than a conversion of the heart is a loss. So, proving your scholarship or eloquence may win you points for style, but the only points that matter are the ones that bring the prodigal closer to Christ. Fighting to the death intellectually may even kill the relationship, which will only make finding God harder if you are one of your child's only reminders of the reality of God. There's a dark joy in beating someone in intellectual combat. It seems as if you're instructing the ignorant, but if your words or demeanor lack mercy, you will likely push your child even further from the Faith. Beating down the values or moral thinking of another person does not result in a conversion of the heart.

Evangelization of a "None" or someone who is on the outer fringes of faith requires us to meet and walk with that person where he or she is, rather than backing the person mentally into a corner with well-crafted rhetoric. It doesn't mean it isn't frustrating as all get-out, and it doesn't mean you shouldn't discuss weighty issues. But the goal should always be to inform, not necessarily to convince. This is not a battle of the titans; this is an attempt to witness and reveal to your prodigal the cause of your joy, the reason for your faith, and the thinking behind your values as manifested in your life.

It is a sublimation of the self to forgo the intellectual battle to witness. The final victory, I promise, will be far more delightful and sublime than any momentary triumph of rhetoric. If you need further convincing to lay down your mental equivalent of a sword, remember that God became man to save the lost sheep. God took on our weakness, our frailty, our limitations, so that our sins might be forgiven. "He will not break a bruised reed or quench a smoldering wick" (Matt. 12:20). We must act similarly and trust that Christ works through His Church to restore each of us fully.

Some wounds are deeper than we have the capacity to heal, save with grace, and it is hard to wait for that grace to reveal itself. Some of us will have birthdays and Christmases and Easters with someone missing from the table, no matter what we do. It is a great pain, and it will weigh on us as nothing else can weigh.

You think it's hard having a child leave the Faith, until you have a child leave both the Faith and your presence. Their absence is an agony for as long as it lasts, and, in some cases, it is years. During such times, hope seems like folly. Prayers feel empty, and all the stories of prodigal children coming home sound like wishful thinking. Saint Monica praying for years offers no comfort, nor does the long suffering of any saint, for it is our children we love, our children we miss, our children we wish would return to us with smiles. We're the ones doing the missing, and while we know the ending of the story for Saint Monica's son, we don't know it yet for our own sons and daughters. It's part of why we pray, "Jesus, I trust in You." As we meditate on the Chaplet of Divine Mercy, we might be tempted to despair. We mustn't. With God, all things are possible, and God is the only one who can bring about the seemingly impossible.

So, pray for your child; pray to see your child one day at the great wedding feast, and trust, again, that Christ is out seeking all of His lost sheep and working to bring each of us home on His shoulders for a seat at the great table. This life—this trial—will not go on forever, but our love will, despite everything, despite all the things that the world and Satan throw at us.

Your Prodigal's Absence May Allow You to Be More Present

One Christmas, after my child left the Church, everyone in my family came to Mass. It isn't that I've not been present at other Masses, but at this celebration of the Eucharist, I couldn't stop smiling and crying at the same time. My heart, for that blessed hour, felt full to the point of overflowing. I didn't want the Mass to end because I didn't want the experience of having all my family together in that sacred place to end.

We know that the celebration of the Mass is the wedding feast of Heaven and Earth, and that's why we celebrate. That's why the early Christians would die rather than not attend, willingly risking their lives to celebrate it. Having everyone at that Mass was a consolation for me, food for the journey. I know that if my child reconciles with the Church in my lifetime such that we come together in that fashion again, it will be another experience of the same type of joy, only greater.

Forgive your prodigal for leaving, and offer prayers for him or her before the Blessed Sacrament, in your heart during the Consecration at Mass, and through little sacrifices every day. Your prodigal's absence will force your presence and bring you further than you might have wanted to walk toward Christ. You now participate in Christ's sufferings. He knows your pain, because it is His own. He thirsts for souls, and you also thirst.

Don't tell yourself it isn't pain; don't pretend it doesn't hurt; and don't refuse your suffering. Instead, as a wise priest said, "Suffer well." Pray for others who know the same pain, and pray for those who won't pray. The phrase "Offer it up" doesn't quite capture the reality of what it is that you do when you unite your sufferings with Christ. Uniting your agony of not having your child in the Church with Christ is to participate in His Passion. It's not easy, but it does bring unique graces, such as the gift of true peace, which has nothing to do with whether or not there is a lack of friction or suffering in your home.

Beauty Will Save the World

There will be hard, dark days and nights of the soul, and, again, the one comfort I can offer is that Jesus knows this agony even more intimately than you do. Hold on to the knowledge that He's doing something about it because He loves the ones we love better than we ever can. When we suffer out of love, we begin to understand how Jesus felt on the Cross and how Mary experienced the piercing of her heart. We begin to grasp how painful our separation from God is to God Himself. Instead of diminishing our faith, it should make us hold all the tighter to it. When we suffer, we share in God's pain, we participate, and that sort of suffering can be, if we accept God's grace, sacrificial and redemptive. It is not easy, but it is holy.

Hold on to God. Hold on to hope. Hold on to beauty. "Beauty will save the world," wrote Dostoyevsky. We will need beauty both as food for ourselves and for those around us to get through this earthly life. Why? Because beauty is a physical manifestation of God's love, which is infinitely beautiful. Wherever our prodigals are in their journey, we must always seek to love them more and more as God loves them, more perfectly, more beautifully. Be fed by beauty, and feed others that same gift.

How?

By living out the beautiful words of the Beatitudes. They are the means by which the anger and the hurt that led your prodigal away can be soothed. When dealing with one you love, whose soul is gravely injured by the past, by bad decisions, by sin, by fear, by poor influences, begin by handling him as you would a newborn. Feed him, keep him warm, keep him safe, and say "I love you." Reflect the goodness and beauty of God by practicing the Beatitudes.

If your adult child is at home and you still have younger children you are raising, remind your prodigal that, as an adult, he or she must be respectful of your values and not undermine your work in raising your other children. If the prodigal lives elsewhere, and it is his or her lifestyle that is antithetical to the Faith, continue to invite that child to your events (cookouts, beach trips, lunch, and so forth), following the example of Christ in Scripture, who doesn't demand that sinners cease sinning to meet Him. Rather, because those who meet Him come to love Him, they cease to sin. Christ doesn't slam doors. He stands at slammed doors and knocks.

If your children ask, "Why doesn't So-and-so go to Mass?" the answer is straightforward: "As adults, people make independent decisions about their lives." Let them know that God respects our free will to opt not to obey and that it's a real act of love on God's part to let us constantly refuse Him and still ask again and again and again for our company. We must do the same.

In the meantime, be kind to yourself. Pray. Eat. Rest. Spend time with good books, good friends, and in the presence of God's beauty (creation) and in God's direct loving gaze before the Blessed Sacrament. You will need the sacraments and you will need others with you to weather this time. You will need, if not a spiritual director, a spiritual support system of prayer warriors, both for yourself and your child.

It's not that you need air all the arguments, discussions, or divisions within your family life, but do ask people to pray for a special intention. You'll find there's a community of people out there, the wounded Body of Christ, willing to pray with you and for you, and to ask you to do the same for them. It's a fellowship, it's a community, it's the Body of Christ. Where one aches, all ache; where one celebrates, all rejoice. The support they give will translate to spiritual strength for you as you walk forward. Still, some days it will hurt, but remember that God will see you through this. It's only how *we* will see this through that is unknown.

The Hope That Is Ongoing

The happy ending of the story in each family, in each of our souls, is like our salvation. It is, but not yet fully. We are part of the community of the Body of Christ, but not yet fully citizens of Heaven. We are pilgrims, seeking our way home, as are all of our prodigals, even if we do not know the way. It is God's story to write. The when of that story is His to orchestrate.

Everyone who loves someone far away from the Faith waits for the day, for that moment of return, and hopes they'll be present when it happens. In my prayer life, I've seen a vision of my prodigal returning, a true smile on her face, and it is something I keep as a treasure and consolation, as a reminder of what I'm praying for, what I'm hoping for. I call that image to mind when things get hard.

Some will explode into the world like the sun with a story of Christ piercing the gray of their hearts and revealing Himself in a moment. Others will return via little graces, day by day, quietly, like leaves in spring returning to a tree. Still others will find Christ in the quiet of their hearts, in service, in loving new people to the point of selflessness, or a combination thereof.

None of us can claim the mantle of sainthood yet. We're still on this side of the veil, and so all of us are either prodigals or in danger of becoming prodigals. We can still muck it up. But we also still have time allotted to us to love better than we have up to now. The story continues, and, provided we cooperate with God's grace, our part in it as lovers of others will never end but will extend into our eternal lives. We will die and be judged and either enter into the Kingdom or, through Purgatory, allow our hearts to be stretched by grace to the point of being able to receive the fullness of joy in Christ's presence. Otherwise, should we refuse all possibility of love and fellowship forever, we will suffer eternal separation from God.

We're aiming for everyone to make it to Heaven. That's God's planned destiny for each of us. It's only our sin that keeps it from being a full reality. Each of us holds a story of a soul we hope will attain that ultimate happiness. Our love for them and the pain that division of faith causes is our participation in the Passion and death of our Lord. If we didn't suffer, we wouldn't actually love. Love is self-sacrifice, and it is revealed by the wants and needs of the other being met by the one who loves. Those who love hurt when their beloved hurts; those who love want because the one they love wants; and the one who loves will surrender everything to heal and help the one they love.

Each of us has people in our lives we want to return to the fullness of the Church. Each of us carries that cross. Each of us knows that Christ does the heavy lifting in that journey to Calvary. He walks with us, day by day, and endures with us, trying to lighten our yoke as much as we will allow. Sooner or later, we find ourselves at the foot of the Cross, where Christ shows us how much He loves the ones we love and how much He loves us, and our hearts will break for the joy and greatness of it.

Not the Final Thoughts

There are no final thoughts to this series of reflections on the struggle to love someone far from the Faith, because there isn't an end to the story for any of us (not yet, anyway). We'd like to think that life steadily progresses and spirals ever upward, but it's got lots of unexpected dips and turns and jumps we won't anticipate and can't plan around. We must simply weather them. We get to be in perpetual advent, a time of blessed waiting for that one day yet to come.

The story of another soul is not something we can fully penetrate. When a person leaves the Faith, it becomes the responsibility of all who love that person to pray for the gifts of the Holy Spirit—for wisdom, understanding, counsel, fortitude, knowledge, piety, and fear of the Lord, and the willingness to exhibit said virtues at all times. Witness and prayer are the strongest tools at our disposal.

In his *Confessions*, Saint Augustine reveals his struggles with the Faith his mother embraces; he does not speak of any struggles his mother may have had with her faith because of her son.

So it is for each of us: we are to seek to console, rather than to be consoled, to understand, rather than to be understood, to love and to serve to the last. When we received these children as infants, we thought our hearts would break with joy, suddenly aware of how much we could love someone we had never seen before. That reality remains, and to our surprise, we can now love even more than we could then because we've loved longer, and we know that we always will.

The best counsel I can give is to be patient. Experienced moms and dads know that you must let a child work at riding a bike. He'll get it in time. Experienced moms and dads know, too, that you must allow your child time to recover when a teenage crush has been crushed. She'll heal. Time is an ally in this journey, but we have to remember, it is God's time, not ours, that matters. Patiently continue to pray for the conversion of their souls. Pray for it in the Rosary, offer your sacrifice for it at Mass, bring the intention with you before the Blessed Sacrament. Ask, hope, and persist.

Each soul is on a great pilgrimage outward and upward, nourished by daily encounters with Christ, and, in turn, drawing other souls into the same journey. We are forever seeking Heaven, whether we know it or not. Our job when it comes to those who are, for whatever reason, outside the Church, is to be a good sign, an outward symbol of an invisible, divine reality. We need to be a sacrament to those who do not avail themselves of the sacraments.

We hope for the day when those we love echo Saint Monica's son: "Late have I loved you, Beauty so ancient and new!"

Prayers to Saint Monica

Exemplary mother of the great Augustine, you perseveringly pursued your wayward son, not with wild threats but with prayerful cries to Heaven. Intercede for all mothers in our day so that they may learn to draw their children to God. Teach them how to remain close to their children, even the prodigal sons and daughters who have sadly gone astray. Amen.

Dear St. Monica, troubled wife and mother, many sorrows pierced your heart during your lifetime. Yet you never despaired or lost faith. With confidence, persistence, and profound faith, you prayed daily for the conversion of your beloved husband, Patricius, and your beloved son, Augustine. Grant me that same fortitude, patience, and trust in the Lord. Intercede for me, dear St. Monica, for (*mention your petition*), and grant me the grace to accept His will in all things, through Jesus Christ, our Lord, in the unity of the Holy Spirit, one God forever and ever. Amen.

The Saint Monica Club

Blessed Monica, mother of St. Augustine, we give
thanks to our Father in Heaven, who looked with
mercy upon your tears over your wayward son. His
conversion and heroic sanctification were the fruit
of your prayers. Dear St. Monica, we now ask you to
pray with us for all those sons and daughters that have
wandered away from God, and to add your prayers
to those of all mothers who are worried over their
children. St. Monica, pray for us. Amen.

Sophia Institute

Sophia Institute is a nonprofit institution that seeks to nurture the spiritual, moral, and cultural life of souls and to spread the Gospel of Christ in conformity with the authentic teachings of the Roman Catholic Church.

Sophia Institute Press fulfills this mission by offering translations, reprints, and new publications that afford readers a rich source of the enduring wisdom of mankind.

Sophia Institute also operates the popular online resource CatholicExchange.com. *Catholic Exchange* provides world news from a Catholic perspective as well as daily devotionals and articles that will help readers to grow in holiness and live a life consistent with the teachings of the Church.

In 2013, Sophia Institute launched Sophia Institute for Teachers to renew and rebuild Catholic culture through service to Catholic education. With the goal of nurturing the spiritual, moral, and cultural life of souls, and an abiding respect for the role and work of teachers, we strive to provide materials and programs that are at once enlightening to the mind and ennobling to the heart; faithful and complete, as well as useful and practical.

Sophia Institute gratefully recognizes the Solidarity Association for preserving and encouraging the growth of our apostolate over the course of many years. Without their generous and timely support, this book would not be in your hands.

www.SophiaInstitute.com
www.CatholicExchange.com
www.SophiaInstituteforTeachers.org

Sophia Institute Press® is a registered trademark of Sophia Institute.
Sophia Institute is a tax-exempt institution as defined by the
Internal Revenue Code, Section 501(c)(3). Tax ID 22-2548708.